£13-95

GW00418003

ARMAGEDDON: 1918

GREAT
WAR
STORIES

ARMAGEDDON: 1918
by Cyril Falls

The Nautical & Aviation Publishing Company of America

copyright © 1964 by Cyril Falls. All rights reserved.

Second edition 1979 published by arrangement with the author's estate.

Printed in the United States of America

Library of Congress Catalog Card Number: 79-90113

ISBN: 0-933852-05-3

Maps drawn by John Carnes

CONTENTS

INTRODUCTION

The final Palestinian and Syrian campaign of World War I is of absorbing interest for several reasons, but most of all because it includes one of the most brilliant cavalry operations in the history of warfare—and the last of its kind. In my view the achievement of the Red cavalryman Budënny in the war against the Whites cannot be ranked with that of Allenby's British cavalry in 1918. The Bolshevik cavalry fought nearly always as mounted infantry and, even when appearing to employ the shock methods of genuine cavalry, was in fact penetrating vast gaps in the front of its overextended and often halfhearted foes.

The future of cavalry was to be in armor, and in the British Army has been perpetuated by cavalry regiments which today form a considerable proportion of the Royal Armoured Corps. Yet to some extent the principles remain. Armageddon illustrates the old truth, still a truth even though armor has on occasion won battles or campaigns largely by itself, that cavalry virtually always has to seize the opportunities made for it by infantry and artillery. In Allenby's victory these were so complete that examples from earlier wars are difficult to find; some would say, leaving Jena aside, all but impossible. Lieutenant-General Bulfin's infantry smashed the opposition so thoroughly, opened so wide a breach, and swept so clean that the three cavalry divisions under the Australian Lieutenant-General Chauvel met practically no opposition until they got behind the Turks—indeed the two divisions which advanced at full strength and without being split up for tasks in aid of the infantry met none at all. It was the infantry which suffered the great bulk of the casualties, those of the Desert Mounted Corps being very small.

This is in no way to belittle the cavalry's role. It did what the commander-in-chief had planned, and the infantry officers were well aware that they would take by far the heavier knocks. Each arm fulfilled its allotted task, and if the leadership and spirit of either had been less good the result would have been far less successful. The offensive would have developed into what the Germans call a *Teilniederlage* (partial over-throw), but would not have resulted in the destruction of the two Turkish armies west of the Jordan or anything near the destruction of the one on the far side. Few precedents are to be found for the extent of this annihilation. In the Franco-Prussian War the French were so completely defeated that their armies in Paris, in and about Metz, and on the Belgian and Swiss frontiers were captured *en masse* or interned by the neutrals; yet at the end of the war they still had a far greater proportion of their forces in the field than did the Turks in Syria after the fall of Damascus. Allenby's superiority of strength was an important factor, but has been somewhat exaggerated. Over thirty years ago I examined the question in the light of all information available, to find that the preponderance was not quite so great as is generally supposed.

I have had at my disposal the official history of the campaign, which I wrote between wars. This is long and detailed, the first volume being devoted to the period of the commands of Generals Sir John Maxwell and Sir Archibald Murray; the second, divided into two parts, to that of Allenby. If I am accused of too persistently quoting myself, I must retort that I should have been a poor military historian indeed if this book were not

quoted here far more than any other. It is pointed out that by
far the larger part of the Turkish papers were destroyed. Some
of those which were captured later disappeared without ever
having been translated. In the late Twenties there was, however, a good deal of information available from senior Turkish
officers who have since died. On one occasion a divisional commander who had served beyond the Jordan came into my room
without an appointment and talked nonstop for over an hour in
excellent French, so clearly and lucidly that I hardly had to slip
in a question. Such contacts are invaluable.

The Germans also lost a lot of documents, though far fewer
because they had much more transport and preserved their
discipline. Their writings on the subject are not, however,
numerous, and the best source for the period is the admirable
account given by the commander-in-chief, General Liman von
Sanders. The British records are good, as they well could be—
the little material sunk by submarines is not missed because the
information is to be found in other sources. The volume of the
Australian official history devoted to Palestine is one of the best
things of its kind I have ever read. Poor Gullet was reaching the
height of his career when he was killed in an air accident as a
member of the Australian Government, just as the Japanese
pressure was beginning to be felt. The number of books in the
bibliography is exceptionally small, but the total literature on
the campaign is not large, and a good few works, especially
regimental histories, were absorbed into the official account.

As regards the Arabs, Liddell Hart's biography of T. E.
Lawrence remains by far the most useful source, largely because it is so thorough and deals with the Arab tactics in general
almost as fully as with the man himself. Next I would put the
study of Lawrence by the Frenchman Beraud-Villars, much
narrower in scope but excellently written and introducing
features of Lawrence's career and personality which could not
well be dealt with when Liddell Hart wrote and which he
would in all probability have shunned at any time. Lawrence's

own writings remain masterpieces. From the literary point of view *The Seven Pillars of Wisdom* is the greater achievement, but I have found myself quoting from *Revolt in the Desert* more often.

The word "battle" took on in the First World War a significance very different from any that it had had before. Battles such as that of the Somme in 1916 and Third Ypres in 1917 continued for months, broken only by pauses for recovery. What is seldom realized is that such titles are popular, though they have triumphed in all circles. Officially there is no such thing as the Battle of the Somme; instead, there is a series of battles, all with appropriate titles which are sometimes forgotten and sometimes remembered. Even Allenby's 1917 offensive at Arras, which lasted just over three weeks, comprised five battles, three bearing the name of the river Scarpe, the other two those of Vimy Ridge and Arleux. In Palestine there are only two official battle titles: Sharon for the fighting in the plain, Nablus for that in the Judaean hills. For the cavalry there are officially no battles, but there are a number of "actions," one "affair," and several "captures," such as that of the stoutly defended village of Samakh. Yet, if the infantry bore the brunt, the main interest on this occasion lies in the exploits of the cavalry.

I hope I may be allowed to add that I know the country well. While preparing to work on the second volume of the official history I spent nearly a month in Palestine and beyond the Jordan. Most of my excursions were made in company with a single armed policeman and on police ponies, because at that time there were virtually only two good roads and quitting a car to investigate scenes of fighting more often than not involved a walk, which was a waste of time. When I returned, I had in my mind every landscape feature of importance. I have never visited Israel, but on the assumption of power by the young King Hussein—one cannot say that he "mounted the throne" or was "crowned" because there was no throne or crown—I returned to Jordan and also revisited the large holding in the Judaean hills and the Old City of Jerusalem which his grandfather had put together while ruler. I can therefore say that I am adequately furnished with geographical knowledge of the terrain.

CYRIL FALLS

Taurus Mountains

TURKEY

Mersin Tarsus Adana Aintab

Killis

Alexandretta

Gulf of Alexandretta

Antioch Aleppo

R. Orontes

Latakia

Hama

CYPRUS

Homs

Mediterranean Sea

VI
Baalbek

Beirut

Sidon R. Litani Damascus

Tyre

Acre

Haifa IV Sea of Galilee
Nazareth Samakh V
Beisan
Jenin
Nablus R. Jordan
Jaffa
Jerusalem Amman

Gaza Dead Sea

Beersheba

Port Said

El 'Arish

Suez Canal EGYPT

SCALE OF MILES
50 0 50 100

John Carnes

Megiddo, 1918 ZERO HOUR, SEPT. 18, WITH POSITION SEPT. 20, 6 P.M.

II

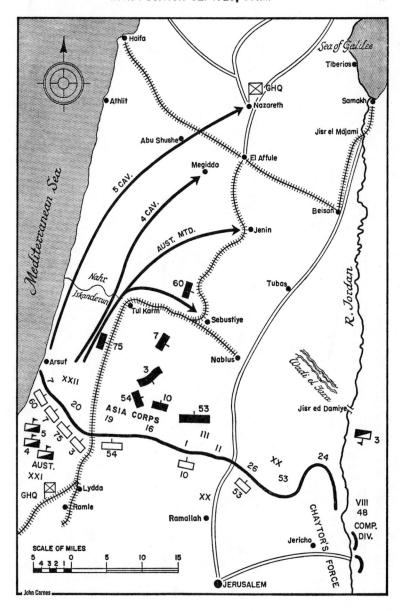

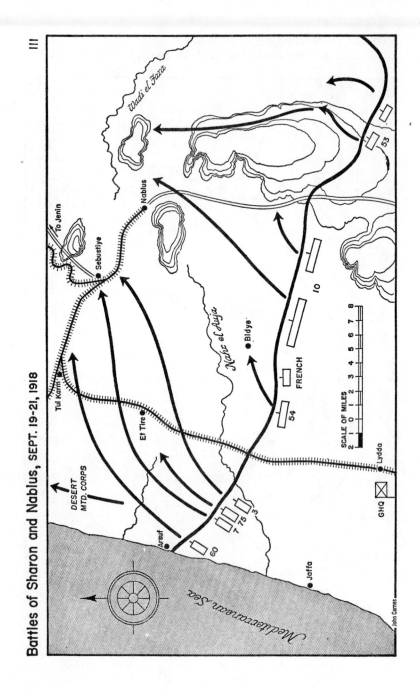

Battles of Sharon and Nablus, SEPT. 19-21, 1918

III

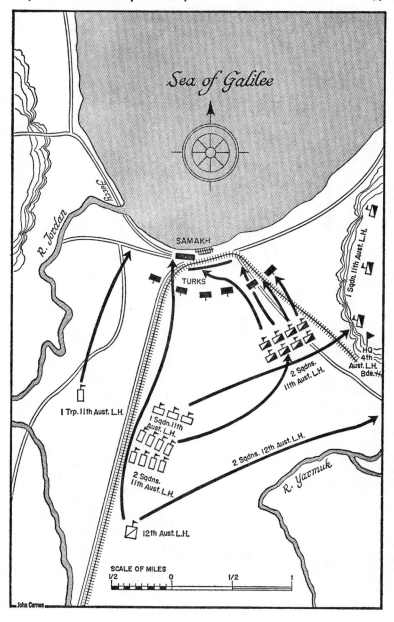

Sea of Galilee

R. Jordan

R. Jordan

SAMAKH

TURKS

1 Sqdn. 11th Aust. L.H.

HQ
4th
Aust. L.H.
Bde.

2 Sqdns.
11th Aust. L.H.

1 Trp. 11th Aust. L.H.

1 Sqdn. 11th
Aust. L.H.

2 Sqdns.
11th Aust. L.H.

2 Sqdns. 12th Aust. L.H.

R. Yarmuk

12th Aust. L.H.

SCALE OF MILES
1/2   0   1/2   1

John Carnes

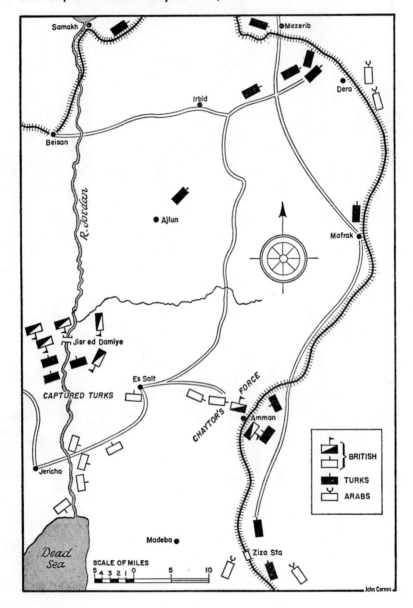

SCALE OF MILES
5 4 3 2 1 0   5   10

John Carnes

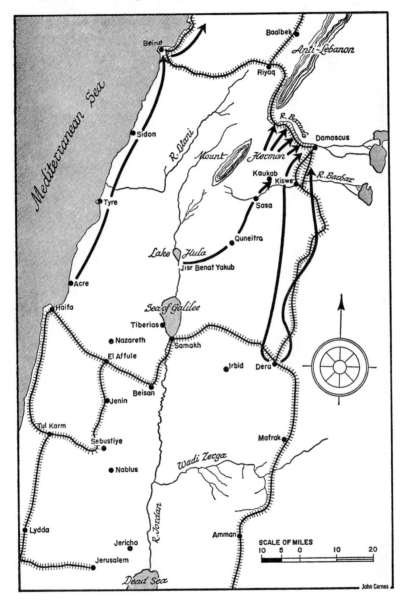

Baalbek

Anti-Lebanon

Beirut

Riyaq

R.Barada

Mediterranean Sea

Sidon

R.Atani

Mount

Hermon

Damascus

Kaukab

Kiswe

R.Barbar

Tyre

Sasa

Acre

Quneitra

Lake Hula

Jisr Benat Yakub

Haifa

Sea of Galilee

Tiberias

Nazareth

Samakh

El Affule

Irbid

Dera

Beisan

Jenin

Tul Karm

Mafrak

Sebustiye

Nablus

Wadi Zerga

Lydda

R.Jordan

Jericho

Amman

SCALE OF MILES
10   5   0   10   20

Jerusalem

Dead Sea

John Carnes

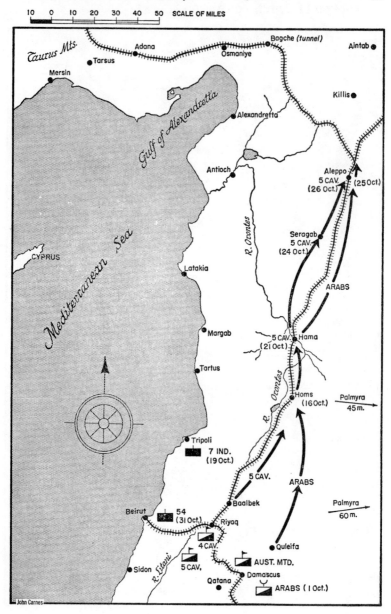

EGYPT, SINAI, AND PALESTINE: THE PAST

1   "ARMAGEDDON" stands for the conflict of nations. Says St. John the Divine, writing in his cell on the island of Patmos: "And they had breastplates, as it were breastplates of iron; and the sound of their wings was as the sound of chariots of many horses running to battle."

The other title by which Allenby's final offensive is known is "Megiddo," from a former town at the mouth of the Musmus Pass where it enters the Plain of Esdraelon. All three of these localities are associated with great captains: Megiddo itself with the victories of Pharaoh Thothmes III and Pharaoh Necho. At Jezreel, in the plain below the slope of Mount Gilboa, Jehu, the great driver, cast the painted Jezebel to the semi-wild dogs, as familiar in modern times as then. Saladin won his crowning glory at the Horns of Hattin. Again on the Jezreel spur, the Mameluke Sultan Kutuz routed the Mongol horde and saved Egypt. Megiddo is a name of power, but Armageddon is even more impressive; it is chosen as the title of this brief history because of its associations and its majesty.

The narrative begins in September 1918, but to understand the situation the shortest possible summary of events is unavoidable. At the opening of the First World War, Turkey did not become a belligerent, but the possibility that she would abandon neutrality was only too patent. Britain's role in Egypt was anomalous. The country was still described as a Turkish province and the British representative as Consul-General. He was in fact absolute ruler. His duties were many, but at the back of them all was his key mission: to keep open the Suez Canal, aptly described by the Germans as the jugular vein of the British Empire.

On October 29, 1914, German warships, the *Goeben* and *Breslau*, forced Russia into the war by bombarding her Black Sea ports, whereupon Britain and France declared war on Turkey on November 5. Early in 1915 the Turks launched a weak offensive on the Suez Canal, relying for success on an internal revolt in Egypt. In that country there was ill feeling against British rule despite the fact it had brought justice and relative prosperity in place of bankruptcy and tyranny.

"It was this prosperity which had altered the point of view of the Egyptians. A new generation had grown up which did not remember the bad old days. No people will for long recognize a foreign power as the source of its well-being."[1] *

The attack on the Canal, which was defended by forces many times greater numerically than the peacetime garrison but for the most part newly raised, was launched on February 3, 1915. On the Turkish side we may call the expedition a brilliant fiasco. It failed to interrupt the traffic in the Canal for more than a few nights and during daylight on the day of the attack. The Turks suffered losses not far short of 2,000 as against 163 British. On the other hand, they had been well led by the German Colonel Freiherr Kress von Kressenstein and had dragged across the desert a little fleet of pontoons, three of which had actually crossed the Canal, though all the men who landed were killed or captured. They had been beaten rather by the fire of the British and French warships moored in the Canal than by the Indian infantry. Primitive French seaplanes had also done good service. The British troops were also ill-equipped, as is shown by the fact that camel convoys to carry

* Superior figures refer to Notes at end of text.

water into Sinai had not been assembled, so that the commander of the force in Egypt, Lieutenant-General Sir John Maxwell, was unable to pursue the retreating Turks.

The desert of Sinai provided, in fact, a formidable buttress against a Turkish attack on Egypt and an even stronger one against a British invasion of Palestine. The Turkish command and its German advisers and technicians also were faced with another obstacle. The single-track railway ran from Haidar Pasha Station on the Bosporus to Riyaq, some 25 miles northwest of Damascus, but it was broken by two great gaps in the Taurus and Amanus mountains, so that troops and supplies had to detrain west of the Taurus gap, move by road to Tarsus, entrain to Alexandretta, take the road again to Aleppo or a station northwest of it, and finally move by rail again to Riyaq. Here, however, their troubles did not end. Riyaq was a primitive station with few facilities for the transfer of goods —especially ammunition and, worse still, coal—to the narrow-gauge line, so that the Turks were soon forced, in a land carrying little timber but for the precious olive, to run their locomotives on wood fuel. The narrow-gauge line bifurcated at Dera, 50 miles south of Damascus, one branch running straight down into the Hejaz and the other to the port of Haifa. The internal rail system of Palestine does not need description, except for one feature which gave the whole thing an air of "Alice in Wonderland": the line from Jerusalem to Jaffa, French owned, was of a gauge slightly different from that of the German-built narrow-gauge sections.

On top of this, the roads were always poor, and the secondary ones abominable. The British and French navies made it impossible to move goods by sea, though an occasional little cargo boat, hugging the shore, may have reached a port as far south as Alexandretta, nearly 400 miles from the southern frontier of Palestine.[2]

Things went relatively quietly for Egypt except for the Western Desert until the Gallipoli campaign, to which General Maxwell had to supply a certain number of reinforcements and take charge of such a multitude of horses and mules not usable on the peninsula that one man had to "do" seven or more a day. After it was over, the evacuated troops poured back, most of them more or less sick, and many wounded from hospitals in the islands of the Aegean. A new command, first known as the Mediterranean Expeditionary Force, later as the Egyptian Expeditionary Force, was set up, and Lieutenant-General Sir Archibald Murray came to take over the duties. Maxwell was left with the charge of internal military duties, including precautions against Egyptian risings and Turkish or German espionage, and to continue operations against the Senussi, the desert sect which was in revolt in the Western Desert.

Murray was one of the handsomest and most soldierlike officers in the British Army, and well versed in staffwork. Up to the eve of war a brilliant military career had been prophesied for him, but had so far not materialized in the field. As chief of staff to Field-Marshal Sir John French on the western front he had been shoved aside by the more vocal, impressive, and—an important factor in view of the terrific strain of the retreat from Mons—physically tougher Henry Wilson, his deputy. Then he had been a success in a brief period as chief of the Imperial General Staff at the War Office. Despite many good qualities, Murray had proved a misfit in the two battles of Gaza—above all in the second.

Meanwhile there had been a highly comic battle of military appreciations. The British defeat on the Gallipoli Peninsula had set free a great number of Turkish troops. Where would they go? The obvious answer was: a handful to fight the Austrians, a considerable number to the Caucasus to fight the Russians, and the remainder divided between Syria and Palestine on the one hand, and Mesopotamia on the other. But how many could be mustered for a general attack—unlike the first, which had been conducted by 20,000 men—on Egypt? Here the Cassandras lacerated themselves and cried "Woe! Woe!" The estimates reached something between two and three hundred thousand men.[3] This was completely ludicrous; there were not that number of Turks south of the Taurus, and in any case nothing like that number could march across Sinai, even in the winter when the wells would be full.

However, the first preparations were based on these most pessimistic assumptions. The first steps taken had much to be said for them, since to defend the Suez Canal and use it as a moat was not desirable. The line was pushed out over ten thousand yards to the east. Vast numbers of Egyptian laborers and a considerable number of troops were employed in fortification, and by January 1916 nearly ten thousand men were on road-making alone. Then, as regards troops, a host was mustered, numbering fourteen divisions in all, though two Australian divisions were not formed in the country until several others had left it. One division was actually brought out from the United Kingdom.

As soon as Murray's successor at the War Office, the hard-minded and practical "ranker," General Sir William Robertson, had taken over as chief of the Imperial General Staff, he ruthlessly cut the estimate of the number of Turks who could cross the Sinai to the figure of a hundred thousand. This, in fact, represented the highest Turkish hopes, but was beyond the enemy's capabilities. Had such an advance taken place, it would undoubtedly have been led by Kress von Kressenstein, though the nominal commander-in-chief was Jemal Pasha, the former Minister of Marine. Robertson acted quickly. He dispersed the great British force in Egypt so that six divisions were gone before the end of the first quarter of 1916 and four more before the end of the second quarter. However, in addition to his four infantry divisions Murray was left with a large force of British Yeomanry, Australian Light Horse, and New Zealand Mounted Rifles.

Meanwhile Maxwell had been busy dealing in the Western Desert with the Senussi, coaxed into the war by Turkish exhortations and gold. They were not a tribe but a nomad sect, headed by a chief named Sayed Ahmed, unexpectedly formidable because he had at his disposal a plump but highly efficient young Baghdadi Arab, Jafar Pasha el Askeri, who had passed through the Turkish military school and served in the German army. Jafar brought the tribesmen up to a remarkable pitch of efficiency; in fact, at the first clash, when he encountered raw Territorial troops, he scattered them. Maxwell, owing to difficulties of communication, was actually forced to abandon Sollum, which raised the spirit of the dissidents. Some of Maxwell's handicaps are illustrated by the fact that in the war diary of one of his columns messages are marked "by flag," which meant that it signaled back through a series of flag stations by dot-and-dash. He was fortunate in that he had at his disposal a large proportion of mounted troops, first Yeomanry only; then, after the Gallipoli campaign, Australian Light Horse as well.

It was the Yeomanry that virtually decided the issue. A dashing charge at Agagiya by the Dorset Yeomanry on February 26 ended with the capture of Jafar, who had been seriously wounded. Never again did the Senussi await a British charge. The incident marked a turning point in the campaign. Maxwell was now ordered home and his separate force ceased to exist.

Murray's shift from pessimism was startlingly swift and complete. From anxiety about a Turkish advance when he had at his disposal a very large force, he went over to the strategy of a British advance across Sinai to the frontier at Rafa though he had now only four infantry divisions. His reasoning was that, if the Turks were to make any dangerously strong effort against Egypt, they must move through Kossaima and El 'Arîsh—the former inland and nine miles from the border, the latter on the coast and twenty-five miles inside Sinai—or else between the two; therefore Egypt could best be defended by occupying this frontage, which covered a little over fifty miles. He did not contemplate a swift advance in the style of Napoleon and other great captains who had traversed the coast route from remote ages. His movement would be accompanied by a railway and a pipeline carrying water, with storage tanks, batteries of standpipes, and a movable reservoir holding 500,000 gallons. It looks pedestrian and has been derided by some critics, but he could hardly have brought his force across the desert otherwise. Twentieth-century British soldiers, as hardy as any Europeans outside Russia and the Balkans, are not so hardy as the ancient Egyptians or even as the troops of Napoleonic France; nor can they long subsist on brackish well water like the Turks.

Murray had one more serious riposte to face when he was attacked at Rumani on August 4, 1916, by the redoubtable Kress at the head of 16,000 troops, including a German battalion of heavy and medium artillery and a machine-gun battalion. Murray's own strength was considerably greater, but limited by water supply. The Turks fought magnificently, but were routed with a loss of nearly 4,000 prisoners, as against a British loss of 202 killed, 882 wounded, and 46 missing. Finally, after two sparkling actions—Magdhaba on December 23 and Rafa on January 9, 1917—in which Turkish outpost garrisons were virtually annihilated, he was able to report to Robertson that he had established himself on the projected line. It is astonishing to contemplate how costs for a little expedition such as this had risen by the first quarter of the twentieth century, though we cannot discover the wage bill for the Egyptian laborers who laid the railway, or even the price of the locomotives bought in the United States.

In February 1914 Lord Kitchener, then still Consul-General in Cairo, had been visited by Emir Abdullah, the second son of the Sherif of Mecca, who informed him of his father's ambition to free the Hejaz from the Turks. On the day the Ottoman Empire entered the war a message was sent to Abdullah by Kitchener's order, assuring the Sherif that Britain would provide active aid. Britain had three motives: the interests of the annual pilgrimages from India, countering the influence of the Turkish *jihad* (proclamation of holy war against infidels), and genuine sympathy for the Arabs. Unfortunately, she complicated her policy by simultaneously arranging with France in the notorious Sykes-Picot Agreement that the latter's interests in Syria should be supported. These interests conflicted with the promise to the Sherif concerning Palestine, and neither negotiator knew what the other was doing. In 1917 Britain was to introduce a further complication, the Balfour Declaration, which promised the Jews a "national home" in Palestine. British policy looks dishonorable in the extreme, but stupidity and lack of co-ordination were most to blame.[4]

On June 5, 1916, revolt broke out in Mecca and the small Turkish garrison was overwhelmed. The summer station of the Turks at Taif, 70 miles to the southeast, surrendered to Abdullah on September 22, after being shelled for two months by two Egyptian pack batteries under their own Moslem officers, which had been sent by the Governor-General of the Sudan, General Sir Reginald Wingate. Though further success was delayed, this was a good start.

The most remarkable of the handful of officers sent to assist the Sherif was Captain T. E. Lawrence, an archaeologist aged twenty-eight, who had worked in Palestine before the war. He was a brilliant but unorthodox natural soldier and later became a great writer. His narratives must, however, be accepted with caution, since he ocasionally exaggerated without shame or scruple. An officer tells us that Lawrence showed him some notes on the miracle produced by striking a rock and bringing forth water; Lawrence had written that he had seen this done—quite a feasible operation with the aid of hypnotism —and that the stream was "as thick as a man's finger," but the spectator saw him scratch out the word "finger" and substitute "wrist." Yet the basis of his writings is as true as it is fascinating and inspiring. He was a man of genius.

Lawrence's first notable exploit was the capture of Wejh, between four and five hundred miles north of Mecca, on January 23, 1917, though the place was actually seized by a body of Arabs landed from British ships. The main body was nominally commanded by the Emir Feisal, the Sherif's third son. This success gave the Arabs a port outflanking the Hejaz Railway, terminating at Medina, and made it virtually impossible for the Turks to recover Mecca. Medina, defended by a fiery old Turkish soldier, proved impregnable and held out till after the war. After the two battles of Gaza had been fought, Lawrence won a smashing victory near 'Aqaba, at the head of the gulf of the same name, and on July 6, 1917, after the garrison had come out and surrendered, entered the valuable though completely undeveloped port.

Meanwhile a new Prime Minister, David Lloyd George, had taken office, and an extraordinary three-sided battle had begun between him, Robertson, and Murray. Lloyd George wanted an offensive in Palestine, indeed anywhere but on the western front. Robertson did not favor one, but he was the Prime Minister's servant and had to obey after pointing out the difficulties, which he did so gloomily that Lloyd George came to dislike the very sight of him. Murray realized the risks even better than Robertson, but was rather more optimistic. Even though one of his four infantry divisions had been withdrawn, he had for some time been considering the possibility of capturing Gaza, a port and fortress twenty miles within the Palestinian frontier. His weakness in infantry was partly atoned for by his strength in mounted troops. Under the command of Lieutenant-General Sir Philip Chetwode he had formed the "Desert Column," consisting of two mounted divisions of four brigades apiece. The command of all the fighting troops was vested in "Eastern Force" under Lieutenant-General Sir Charles Dobell. The desert was now left behind—which made the title of the force incongruous—and a considerable reorganization, including the substitution of wheeled vehicles for camels in the transport of the infantry divisions, had been approved by the War Office. The pipeline had now reached El 'Arîsh and the railway beyond it.

Gaza had been called a fortress, but it was an improvised one. Its capture presented two difficulties: forcing a way through the Turkish trenches and immense cactus hedges surrounding it, and finding water for the horses, without which the cavalry would have to return at nightfall. The cavalry's role was to swing round the defenses on ridges running in a southwesterly direction. The town was then to be taken by a *coup de main*, while the infantry held off the Turks, whose main body was certain to come from the east. The advance on March 6, 1917, was delayed by dense fog, but the work of the guides was so good that the assault started almost up to time.

The troops were in good heart and proved successful in capturing three successive objectives along the ridges. As dusk fell, the cavalry reached the northern and eastern fringe of Gaza and actually penetrated the town.

Meanwhile the energetic Kress had been driving his troops to arrive for the rescue, hoping to have two divisions in action near Gaza before the fall of darkness, but had been hindered by "typically Turkish" delays before they could be got on the move, so that they constituted no real threat that day. If the Turks were slow, the British were muddle-headed. The cavalry was recalled, though it had found large rain pools at which a number of the horses had been watered. An error about the situation of an infantry division led to a needless abandonment of ground. The infantry was withdrawn the next day. So that what should have been a success became a defeat with casualties of 523 killed, 2,932 wounded, and 412 missing, whereas the enemy's losses amounted to 301 killed, 1,085 wounded, and 1,061 missing, figures which included 57 Germans and Austrians.

Murray next committed an unforgivable sin in sending home a misleading telegram which induced Robertson to believe a victory had been won and brought a congratulatory telegram from King George V. One incredible sentence ran: "The operation was most successful and owing to the fog and waterless nature of the country round Gaza just fell short of a complete disaster to the enemy." The consequence was that Robertson, anxious to fulfill the wishes of the new Prime Minister, David Lloyd George, though personally not keen on the campaign, pressed Murray to resume the offensive, which Murray personally was loath to do.[5]

The situation was now altogether changed and it was no longer a question of cutting out Gaza. The troops brought up by Kress had not gone back to their quarters; in part they had been placed in a perimeter of defenses south of the city; in part they were working as few but Turkish peasants can work in constructing redoubts along the high road running southeast to Beersheba. There would thus have to be a purely frontal attack, but where? The dunes between Gaza and the sea were ruled out because the going was heavy. This was a serious mistake, since to the Gaza–Beersheba road, across the ground on which barley dear to Scottish distillers was grown, was a glacis as perfect as Vauban himself could have contrived and far more extensive.

The offensive, beginning on April 17, failed completely, despite the aid of a handful of ancient tanks, with heavy loss and fearful slaughter in the division which had the main task in the advance against the road. For the most part the Turks sat in their redoubts and shot the division to pieces. In four days the British losses numbered 509 killed, 4,359 wounded, and 1,576 missing. Of these the division mentioned, the 54th, suffered an over-all loss of 2,870—one of its brigades lost 1,828, which meant that it was temporarily destroyed as a fighting formation. In the same period the Turkish loss was only 402 killed, 1,364 wounded, and 245 missing. Murray sacked Dobell, but his own doom was not to be long delayed. On June 11 he was informed by Robertson that a change in command was desired by the Government. This capable man had brought most of his troubles upon his own head. He had made his general staff a military secretariat pure and simple and had kept his headquarters in Egypt, as though the Canal defenses and the Western Desert were almost as important as Palestine. His successor, General Sir Edmund Allenby, arrived in Cairo on June 27, 1917.

The new commander-in-chief came out under a slight cloud because the Battle of Arras, though starting splendidly with the greatest success yet won, had ended in bloody deadlock, after involving a formal written protest from three of his generals.[6] He was a tall, heavy cavalryman with an explosive temper, a combination which had earned him his nickname of "The Bull," but also he had a great personality, and inspired enthusiasm. T. E. Lawrence said of him: "His mind is like the prow of the *Mauretania*. There is so much weight behind it that it does not need to be sharp like a razor." He found an army dispirited by defeats which it felt it had not deserved,

and transformed it in a matter of weeks into one eager to fulfill all its new leader's behests, however difficult. Allenby was,
in his spare time, a good botanist and ornithologist and highly
observant. In South Africa this quality had staved off a minor
disaster. Riding toward a farm to buy poultry and eggs, he
saw through his glasses that the stone wall was lined with
ducks, and said to his companion: "Did you ever see ducks
perching on a wall before?" He then turned back and ordered
the squadron behind him to retire. Directly this movement
began, a hot musketry fire broke out from a party of Boers
behind the wall, who had put the ducks there as a trap.[7]

Critics of the conduct of the war on the western front,
basing their arguments on the enormous casualty lists, often
proclaim that the leaders were incompetent. When it is pointed
out to them how many British, French and, above all, German generals served there and on other fronts as well, they
retort that these generals were poor generals in France and
Belgium and good ones elsewhere. This is unadulterated rub-
bish, the truth being that, because all the belligerents regarded
the western front as the principal one, the proportion of troops
and artillery to miles was by far the greatest, so that it was far
harder to open a wide breach. Yet there is a sense in which
Allenby's skill was greater in his new command than in those
he had previously held. First of all, he had an intense love for
being boss and delighted in an independent command. Then,
though he did not dislike Field-Marshal Sir Douglas Haig,
commander-in-chief since December 1915, he was always ill at
ease in Haig's presence. Some said that one of the reasons was
petty. At the staff college—where Haig was brilliant and he
very much the reverse—he had been elected Master of the
Drag Hounds, though Haig was a beautiful horseman and
Allenby no more than a competent hard rider. This judgment,
again, may be far from the truth, but trifling rivalries sometimes live on in the minds of men whom one would expect to
be above them.

Allenby's most successful appointment before the war had
been that of Inspector-General of Cavalry. Those who had

expected when he came to visit them that his tone would be hectoring and that he would find faults in their conduct of training were agreeably surprised to find him calm and helpful, though clear in pointing out what he considered to be mistakes.

Now, like nearly all men in such circumstances, Allenby demanded reinforcements . . . and got them. Actually the nuclei of two divisions, one of dismounted Yeomanry and the other on the Indian establishment of three Indian battalions and one British battalion per brigade, were for the most part already in the country. The third division came from Macedonia. Allenby shifted his headquarters to the front and formed two corps under Chetwode and a newcomer, Lieutenant-General Sir E. S. Bulfin. He possessed the resources to increase the cavalry, now known as the Desert Mounted Corps and commanded by the Australian Lieutenant-General Sir H. G. Chauvel, to three divisions. The strength of the Turkish Army had increased on paper to a similar extent and now numbered three corps, totaling eight divisions west of Jordan, but these divisions were much smaller than the British.

Allenby's plan, adumbrated by Chetwode, was to roll up the enemy's front from Beersheba after capturing it and its all-important wells. Before this stroke on his right he intended to begin a systematic bombardment of the Gaza defenses on his left and at the most suitable moment to assault those between the city and the coast. This attack was to be a feint.

Beersheba was duly captured, the final stroke being a charge by an Australian brigade, the men—good riders but not cavalrymen—carrying bayonets for effect, a magnificent exploit. The wells were secured, but the Turks had been given ample time to destroy them had they possessed the initiative, and Allenby and Chetwode have been blamed for counting on securing them intact. Then matters began to go wrong. The cavalry became unduly dispersed and was handicapped by the adverse factor of insufficient water supply, which dogged the Egyptian Expeditionary Force from first to last, though even then it took large numbers of prisoners. Allenby was not perturbed. He turned his feint into the real thing, broke through to the coast, swept up the coast road, disregarding pin pricks from the Turks on his right flank, wheeled into the Judaean hills, and on December 9, after prolonged and hard fighting, captured Jerusalem. Lloyd George's somewhat amateurish demand for the Holy City as a Christmas present had been fulfilled, but not cheaply, the casualties being about 18,000. However, the casualties of the enemy were 25,000, nearly half again as large.

As for the Turks, Jemal Pasha had departed in high dudgeon, as had Kress von Kressenstein, whose dispositions at Third Gaza had not satisfied Turkish senior officers. Though the German was by far the abler soldier, the departure of the Turk was in one respect more damaging. There had been some talk of retaining him as Inspector-General, Lines of Communication, but the post was not lofty enough. Major-General Ali Fuad Pasha, commanding the Turkish XX Corps, had remarked to Kress: "Now we shall go hungry, because Jemal will have no interest in feeding us."[8]

The enemy was now commanded by one of the greatest soldiers of the war, General (Marshal in the Turkish army) Erich von Falkenhayn, the former chief of the German General Staff and later the conqueror of Rumania. He had actually been sent out to undertake a grandiose scheme concocted by the Turkish Minister of War, Enver Pasha, and typical of his impracticable dreams. At the head of a Turkish army of fourteen divisions and a German contingent six thousand strong, he was to recover Baghdad. The project, known as Yilderim ("Lightning" in Turkish), was crazy, as he soon discovered. Though stopgap narrow-gauge railways had been cut through the Taurus and Amanus mountain ranges, such a force could be neither transported to nor maintained in Mesopotamia. In any case the situation in Palestine was by now far graver from the Turkish point of view. Falkenhayn had not reached the scene when Allenby attacked, but he displayed first-class leadership in the fighting north of Jerusalem. The leading divisions of the Yilderim Army Group were engaged, but Falkenhayn could not muster sufficient force to retake Jerusalem. His counteroffensive was defeated with almost contemptuous ease by Chetwode, who, before the year was out, attacked in his turn and won ground enough to make his hold on the city secure.

Disorganized as the Turks now were, Allenby could not follow up his advantage. Rains such as octogenarian Arabs with wagging white beards asserted they had never seen before flooded the land and swept away bridges and culverts. Allenby was literally bogged down and lost a wonderful chance by only a few weeks. In March he launched a raid beyond Jordan which was defeated; then followed it up by a second in April which met with a like fate. He was not altogether candid in describing these two operations as "raids," because he had meant to retain most of the ground won, including Amman on the Hejaz Railway and Es Salt. A spring offensive in Palestine to which he was looking forward was denied to him.

March 21, 1918, was indeed a black day for the British in France, and the prelude to a distressing and extremely dangerous defeat. The British Government and the War Office had been perfectly well aware that it must come because they had full information about German troop movements since the Russian revolution and the Treaty of Brest-Litovsk and knew that there were 194 German divisions on the western front, with more to come. They should have begun to reduce the Egyptian Expeditionary Force at least a month earlier than they actually did. Allenby now sent back two divisions, the infantry strength of two more, several batteries and machine-gun companies.

Actually his strength was to be raised to what it had been before, though in the greater part of the infantry the quality was inferior. Two good Indian divisions were sent from Mesopotamia, but the Indian battalions which filled up the rest—except for one kept all British in case there came another call from France—were very raw. In some cases not a junior British officer spoke Hindustani and hardly an Indian officer even understood English. These troops, however, were considerably improved by their summer training. On the other hand, Allenby's cavalry was greatly strengthened. Two Indian cavalry divisions were sent from France without the British regiment per brigade, this latter being replaced by Yeomanry already available. A French cavalry regiment of Spahis, sent to show the flag, proved excellent in every engagement, its only weakness being that its good-looking and enduring Arab horses and kindred barbs from North Africa could not keep pace with the big Walers of the Australian brigade to which it was attached. The Desert Mounted Corps now consisted of the 4th and 5th Cavalry Divisions, the Australian Mounted Division, and the Australian and New Zealand (ANZAC) Mounted Division. The Australian Mounted Division was, at its own request, trained with the sword, but the Australian and New Zealand Division, which was to fight beyond Jordan in its old role of mounted infantry, did not follow the example.

Meanwhile the Arabs under Feisal and Lawrence had left the Hejaz far behind. Their policy, never consciously acted upon—though Lawrence would have us believe otherwise—but representing their resources, was to keep the Hejaz Railway barely working but no more and the Medina garrison bottled up. This was carried out by frequent raids on the railway, blowing up the line, especially at bridges. A semi-regular force was formed under Jafar Pasha, who had voluntarily changed sides in face of Turkish barbarity to the Arab peoples. Another notable Arab figure was Nuri Bey, a still younger man, who acted as Feisal's chief of staff. Both were to serve as prime ministers of Iraq, and both were fated to die at the hands of assassins. For the autumn offensive a "British Section," including Egyptian Camel Corps, a French artillery detachment, and Jafar's brigade, was formed. Bedouin were recruited as need arose and lavishly paid with golden sovereigns. These canny sons of the desert did not believe in paper money and the war proved for them a generally attractive deal. The fellahin were also paid, but they ran the risk of having their villages burnt and their wives and children slaughtered by the Turks. One feature of this lavish support of the Arabs which never appears in British official documents, still less in books published later, is that a large amount of the gold found its way into Turkish pockets.[9]

In other respects Allenby's striking power was strengthened. On April 1, 1918, the naval and military air forces were amalgamated as the Royal Air Force, an air ministry having been set up in the previous January. Major-General W. G. H. Salmond was General Officer Commanding, Middle East, but regarded Palestine as his primary theater. In theory Allenby could not issue orders to him, since the RAF was independent; in practice he accepted the commander-in-chief's proposals as instructions, just as his brother John accepted those of Field-Marshal Haig on the western front. The Palestine Brigade, RAF, under the command of Brigadier-General A. E. Borton, was entirely at Allenby's disposal. Earlier in the campaign the Germans had dominated the air by a simple but effective policy: however scanty the aid they could give to the Turkish theaters, they provided a handful of up-to-date fighters. This superiority was now a thing of the past.

The Palestine Brigade consisted of two wings, in all seven squadrons, of which one was Australian. It included Bristol fighters and one giant Handley-Page, which could carry sixteen 112-lb. bombs and remain in the air for eight hours, flown by Captain Ross Smith, who was to make the first flight from England to Australia in 1919. This force gave Allenby complete mastery of the skies. One of its functions was the brilliant and unceasing support of Lawrence's Arabs, who would have been well-nigh helpless without it for the bolder enterprises in which they were to engage. The forces at Allenby's disposal were for the first time well balanced in all respects and the Germans now found themselves outfought in the air. The best service was rendered by the Australian Flying Corps, which had eighteen Bristol fighters as well as the Handley-Page.[10]

The only troops not in good fighting condition were the Australians and New Zealanders, who had been kept in the blazing Jordan Valley to deceive the enemy into the belief that the next thrust would be to Amman and up the Hejaz Railway. There they encountered shade temperatures ranging from 100 to 120 degrees Fahrenheit, with exceptional humidity, owing to the extraordinary evaporation from the Dead Sea. Mosquitoes, centipedes, and stinging spiders were their bedfellows, and the majority suffered from malaria and minor recurrent fevers. They were "gaunt ghosts" and "poor as crows," and their horses were in low condition from picking up sand with their scanty feed.[11]

WAITING FOR THE WHISTLE

2   THE ROLE OF CAVALRY had long been in decline. Gone were the days when it could hope to break unshaken infantry, as it had done so often in the Thirty Years' War. In the present conflict cavalry had proved valuable in the early stage of open warfare in France but since the front had become congealed it had known few successes except in defense, until the German offensive in March 1917 had brought about a return to fluidity. Then again its task had been chiefly that of patching holes in the infantry array, though it had brought off one spectacular charge which had momentarily eased the pressure.

In Palestine and Syria the cavalry was to be given a magnificent opportunity to wind up its career in success and glory. In the first place, it was well led by experienced and dashing officers, highly trained, and with a record of success which went back to the days of Murray's approach to the frontier—though it had been deprived of a triumph at the First Battle of Gaza by hesitant leadership—and had, in general, continued under Allenby. Then, the proportion of troops to the breadth of the front was small enough to create wide spaces which it could hope to penetrate. The Turkish cavalry was trifling in strength, and the Turkish infantry, lacking adequate transport, was short of food and already considerably discouraged by constant defeat.

There are, nevertheless, a few achievements to the credit of cavalry after the exploits of the Desert Mounted Corps. One began a few days later in Macedonia during the Allied offensive which drove Bulgaria out of the war. A hard-bitten, hard-drinking Frenchman with an immortal name, General Jouinot-Gambetta, carried out a feat which would have been applauded by Chauvel and his divisional commanders, Major-Generals Sir George Barrow, H. J. Macandrew, and H. W. Hodgson. Franchet d'Espèrey, the then commander-in-chief in that theater, drove along the column in his car and ordered Jouinot-Gambetta to change his original direction and make for Skoplje in the Vardar Valley. There, after forced marches, Jouinot-Gambetta rode into the midst of a large force of Bulgarians in full retreat. In theory his force might have been destroyed, but the enemy was demoralized, although some German troops who had by no means lost their spirit were close at hand. This bold action added considerably to the big haul of prisoners taken. On the other hand, Jouinot-Gambetta rode at the head of only three regiments of Spahis and Chasseurs d'Afrique.

Then, in Mesopotamia, Brigadier-General Cassels (later General Sir Robert Cassels, commander-in-chief in India in the earlier part of the Second World War) carried out a somewhat similar feat, and this time after Allenby's campaign was all but over, the offensive having been launched on October 23, 1918. Cassels rode right around the Turks, crossing two difficult fords over the Little Zab and the Tigris in their rear. Being gradually strengthened by more cavalry and by infantry, he managed to hold out through some hard fighting. He was, in fact, the principal architect of the victory of Sharqat and the capture of 11,000 men and 50 guns, since the British infantry had failed to break the enemy's front. However, the strongest force of cavalry under his command was only two brigades.[1]

In 1919 the future Marshal Budënny, an ex-trooper born in the Don Valley but not a Cossack, distinguished himself against the Whites—one British general still speaks of him with respect because of being kicked out of Russia by him. Next year Budënny won successes against the great Polish leader, Marshal Pilsudski, before the latter won his crowning glory in front of Warsaw and saved Europe from Bolshevism. The Russian led a "cavalry army" of four divisions in the Polish campaign, a greater force than Allenby's if we exclude the division which fought east of the Jordan as mounted infantry. Budënny might therefore be called the leader of the last great exploit by cavalry. His skill and personality inspired his troops in their advance over virtually desert country to Tsaritsyn— which has changed its name twice since, having been known as Stalingrad until recently. On the other hand, there is something unrealistic in his victory over the Whites. Their leaders were incompetent, except for the flamboyant Baron Wrangel. Often and often the troops of both sides merely went through the motions of fighting and, as in the Thirty Years' War, enlisted on the victorious side after they had been captured. On balance the claim for Allenby must stand. However demoralized the Turks became they always meant to fight, though this does not apply to the Arab troops in their ranks.

Falkenhayn's departure had followed that of Jemal "the Great." In early March Allenby learned that Falkenhayn had been succeeded by the cavalryman General Liman von Sanders, who was likewise accorded the Turkish rank of marshal. One of the dismissed commander-in-chief's heaviest handicaps had been his staff, almost entirely German, with very few Turkish linguists, and driven to address the senior officers in French. The staff was often accused of intrigue against Turkey with the aim of securing her railways in Asia and controlling them after the war, but it does not appear that this was widespread. The staff did, however, include one arch-intriguer, Franz von Papen, and he did Falkenhayn a great deal of harm.

Falkenhayn had failed and new blood may have been necessary. In some respects it proved for the good. Liman, since his defense of the Gallipoli Peninsula, was a popular and heroic figure to the Turks. As chief of the German Military

Mission before the war he knew their army thoroughly. He brought a predominantly Turkish staff and had refused to take up his appointment unless allowed to bring with him as chief of staff the Turkish General Kiazim Pasha. The change in command brought about a remarkable change in strategy. Falkenhayn was essentially a man of maneuver, Liman a man of trench warfare. On the peninsula this strategy had been triumphant and Liman did not realize that ground in Palestine lacked the value it had represented there. Falkenhayn had decided on defense in great depth. He had announced his intention to withdraw the Turkish army from its present front ten miles north of Jaffa to the Nahr Iskanderune, which runs through Tul Karm to the sea, a distance of twelve miles. He had sent back the bulk of the general staff from Nazareth to Damascus, and apparently meant to accompany the operations section there a little later. "The staff has already had to clear out at the very last moment, from the Mount of Olives; that must not happen again. The work of the staff must be carried out in a careful and orderly manner, without undue excitement." In that appreciation he proved himself a Cassandra whose warnings were disregarded but nevertheless came true.[2]

Liman canceled the orders; recalled the staff; summoned Jevad Pasha, commanding the Eighth Army, to his old headquarters; and brought back a corps which had crossed the Jordan. One can see what he was driving at, since Falkenhayn had a different blind spot in his failure to realize fully the difficulties of maneuver on bad roads for troops very short of transport, but on balance the new strategy played into Allenby's hands.

The final dispositions of the Turks were as follows: on the right, the coast sector, the Eighth Army, under the command of General Jevad Pasha; in the Judaean hills, the Seventh Army under the already illustrious General Mustapha Kemal Pasha, destined for even greater fame as the Ghazi; beyond Jordan the Fourth Army, under General Mohammed Jemal Pasha "the Lesser." The left-hand corps of the Eighth

Army was entitled the Asia Corps and was commanded by the German *Oberst* von Oppen. In addition to two Turkish divisions Oppen had under his orders the German "Pasha II" contingent, less a regiment east of the Jordan. This was a reinforcement of great value, the equivalent of a division or more, with field and mountain artillery, heavy and light machine guns, and troops picked for fitness. The insensate rivalry between Turks and Germans in the Caucasus after the collapse of Russia had led to orders to withdraw all these, but Liman had, after great efforts, succeeded in retaining them, with the exception of one *Jäger* battalion.[3]

Allenby had a great superiority in strength and especially in cavalry. His force consisted of 12,000 sabres, 57,000 rifles, and 540 guns. He estimated Turkish strength to be 3,000 sabres, 23,000 rifles, and 340 guns, including the Fourth Army but not the 6,000 in the region of Ma'an or a reserve of 3,000.[4] Liman puts the figure still lower. But "rifle strength" did not in Turkish parlance include machine guns, and the Turkish infantry had nearly twice as many of these west of the Jordan as did the British and French infantry. The machine-gun personnel of a division numbered 800, which raises the fighting strength by some 8,000. Again, among the documents shortly to be captured at Liman's headquarters was a strength return of two divisions: ration strength 6,457 and 5,600, rifle strength 2,262 and 1,878. In both cases the rifle strengths were well above the British estimates. Far from Allenby having put the Turkish force too high, it appears that he underestimated it. However, he was overwhelmingly superior in cavalry, as regards both quantity and quality.[5]

Allenby was, indeed, stronger even than these figures show. Mention has been made of cavalry "mounted on horses." The Egyptian Expeditionary Force also possessed highly mobile forces normally working with the cavalry—two light armored motor batteries and two light car patrols, both of which in their several roles proved of value. Allenby had all he could desire—save in one sentimental sense. British cavalry regiments were unrepresented, except by a few officers. How-

ever "the Yeomen of England" took their place, as cavalry and
horse artillery. In the latter capacity they served the Australian
Mounted Division as well as the 4th and 5th Cavalry Divisions.
The Australian troops in this theater had no artillery of their
own, and the Australian and New Zealand Division was supported by British and Indian batteries.

The disparity between the opposing forces in numerical
strength was not nearly so grave from the Turkish point of
view as the disparity of resources and welfare brought about
by the capacity of their respective communications. The
British communications were now first class. Sir George Ma-
cauley, who had retired from the Royal Engineers to enter
the service of the Egyptian State Railways before the war,
was expert in the handling of Egyptian labor, which was hard-
working and cheerful, though timid. The expansion of the
railways had been very great. The rail line across the Sinai had
been doubled to Rafa, and, since the work had been done relatively at leisure, the new line was superior to the original. It
was therefore used exclusively for the heavily loaded down
trains and was carrying over two thousand tons a day. Before
the Third Battle of Gaza the line had been extended closer to
the front. After the battle it was extended to Beersheba, so
that supplies could be unloaded on the road to Jerusalem. From
here to Lydda a standard-gauge line replaced the original narrow gauge. From Lydda to Jaffa the line, which had been
dismantled by the enemy, was also relaid in the standard
gauge. In some sections, in order to use the rolling stock and
locomotives already in the country, trains were made up from
two sets, which was thought to be without precedent in railway history.

The rail network was now as efficient as in any European
theater, including the western front, but the situation had been
bettered to an equal extent by the revolutionary change in the
sources of food and fodder. Allenby's chief administrative
officer (in British parlance Deputy Quartermaster-General, the
"Deputy" not implying that he was a second string but standing for his rank), Major-General Walter Campbell, the canni-

est of Scots, had become largely responsible for the exploitation of the resources of Egypt. A large fishing fleet had been established on Lake Manzala, west of Port Said. These developments and those which followed had been brought about by the increasing threat of German and Austrian submarines in the Mediterranean. The United Kingdom had virtually ceased to be a source of supply. Though a good deal of frozen and preserved meat still came from the United States and the Argentine, and flour from Canada, the bulk of the food followed routes little affected by submarines: from India, Ceylon, Australia, and New Zealand, while Egypt provided all the hay stuffs, fresh vegetables, and sugar. Since the capture of Jaffa unlimited stocks of oranges had been available. Live sheep and goats—indispensable for Indian troops—could be purchased in the country, when not imported from Cyprus. One may in fact say that troops and animals had never had it so good.

The moral comforts and anodynes, on the other hand, were inferior to those in France and Belgium. Home leave, the foremost prerequisite of them all, was almost nonexistent for junior officers and the rank and file, except for a trickle granted on compassionate grounds. Leave to Egypt was given on a considerable scale and camps for leave parties were set up at Cairo and Alexandria. There were, of course, the usual cinema shows and concert parties. Egypt, with its vices, natural and unnatural, was by no means an ideal leave resort and was responsible for most of the venereal disease. Serious riotous disorders also occurred. In particular, the Australians, always as unruly in the back areas of any theater of war as they are well-behaved on campaign, displayed their resentment of cheating and overcharges by beating up the culprits and burning districts where the red lamps were hung out. Their New Zealand cousins also knew how to make their displeasure felt, though they were more sedate in their behavior.

In general the troops were in a high state of fitness in mind and body. Owing to the low casualty rate since the capture of Jerusalem there was no difficulty in keeping up the standard of tactics because the junior officers and noncommissioned officers were not being constantly replaced and the rank and file did not forget the lessons learned. The one serious weakness of the infantry did not matter in Palestine because its habit of walking about on sky lines did not bring from the Turkish gunners the retribution it would have brought from Germans. Divisions and single battalions sent to France started their service there by being severely hammered because of this fault, though otherwise these veterans were to prove themselves to be among the best troops in their new theater.

On the Turkish side the situation was utterly different. The majority of the ministers and the senior officers in Constantinople had largely lost interest in the Palestine campaign. Some of the Young Turks foremost in the revolution in 1908 were Jews, others were only nominally Muslims, like Enver. Their doctrine of Pan-Turanianism, which had replaced Pan-Islamism, was a mystical yearning for the union of "Turanian" races.[6] A close resemblance is to be found in the doctrine of Hitler, in great part derived in a muddled way from Nietzsche. Persian Azerbaijan, Turkestan, and above all Caucasia, filled the vision of the former revolutionaries almost to the exclusion of the Arab possessions of Turkey. One at least of the Turkish army commanders in the theater, Mustapha Kemal, was an out-and-out Pan-Turanian, as he was to reveal after the war in his readiness to shed Arab states and in his tampering with the Mohammedan faith. On the other hand, Kemal was always a professional soldier; whereas Enver, though bred a soldier, was an incorrigible amateur. Kemal recognized that while the war lasted it was urgently necessary to defend Palestine and Syria.

The Turkish army and corps commanders were competent, if slow in their reactions by comparison with the Germans. Liman gives particular praise to Jemal the Lesser and makes no suggestion that he was anti-German, as several British chroniclers have alleged. Lower down in the scale, however, the weakness was grave. The rapid expansion of the forces after the outbreak of war, the enormous losses suffered in the campaigns in Caucasia, the high mortality among the wounded owing to bad surgeons and physicians—all these had led to wholesale promotion of underofficers who were almost always uneducated and often stupid into the bargain. There were few Turkish officers who could not be relied upon to fight stubbornly in entrenched positions, and most of those who had risen from the ranks, having the peasant's instinctive sense of ground, were good at night work; but the majority were incapable of even the simplest maneuver.

The account already given of the enemy's communications will make it clear that the troops were always hungry. They were also ravaged by disease to an enormously greater extent than their foes. They took no precautions against malaria, which prostrated great numbers, and it was mainly infection from their areas that plagued the British. Allenby could to a great extent control his own *Anopheles* mosquitoes, but not those of the Turks or the winds which blew them in; once his offensive started, his troops found themselves amidst the mosquitoes' breeding places. The German doctors, however, did the Allies a good turn by staving off or confining the great scourges of war: cholera, typhus, and bubonic plague.[7] Needless to say, the notorious Spanish influenza, which swept over the world this summer and hit the armies hard, was disastrous for the Turks. In France the British troops affected were nearly all on their feet again in a few days, though things were to be very different when, in the autumn, a more vicious form attacked the United Kingdom, killing a multitude of the old and infirm.

The Turks possessed neither the knowledge nor the means to bring their sick back to health. They were also suffering, when the British offensive started, from the effects of a disaster which had occurred a year earlier.

On September 6, 1917, an explosion at Haidar Pasha Station, opposite Istanbul, had destroyed nearly all the munitions and stores collected for Yilderim. These were at the time destined for Mesopotamia, but over half would have been diverted to Palestine, and their loss was a grave handicap.

There was something mysterious about the affair: though it may have been an accident, it was possibly due to sabotage.

Desertion, also, was a serious problem for the Turks. The number who surrendered to the British was considerable and very useful to them, owing to the information provided. This was, however, only a rivulet by comparison with the torrent which flowed into the back areas of the Turkish lines of communication, where there were actually more deserters than troops serving with the colors, and twenty times as many as gave themselves up. The reason is not far to seek. Deserters who worked on the land in civilian clothes or pillaged supply depots were much better off than the loyal soldiers.

The British, looking at their emaciated captives, supposed that food supplies in northern Palestine and Syria were eaten up, and this impression created anxiety, especially to the cavalry divisional commanders, who realized that their range would be narrowed unless they could live to a considerable extent on the country. (None below them worried because no one had a notion of the depth of the projected advance. The operation order of the XX Corps contained the following passage: "Paragraphs 1, 2, and 3 of these orders are not to appear in any written orders; and only such portions of them will be communicated to Brigade Commanders as is essential for the performance of their tasks." The paragraphs in question spoke of no objective farther north than Nablus.) The cavalry was to be agreeably surprised by the amount of sustenance for men and beasts that could be purchased.

As yet no one was rash enough to expect a walkover. In the open country, British strength, fitness, armament, and superior transport would doubtless prevail, but the Turkish tradition of dour courage and tenacity in trenches commanded general respect; in fact, higher respect than was in this case found to have been warranted. In some instances the Turks lived up to their reputation, but taken as a whole they did not. On the other hand the Germans' achievement was magnificent, but they had plentiful mechanical transport and kept a tight hand on their food supplies.

Two actions heartening from the British point of view took place during the period of waiting and preparation.

The first was a Turkish offensive on the craggy western slope of the Jordan Valley, known as the Affair of Abu Tulul. The position was held by Australian Light Horse, while to the southeast, some six miles away, a brigade of the 5th Cavalry Division covered the Jordan bridges. The enemy's attack was strong and well-planned. He had chosen a point where, despite his general inferiority, he could bring local superiority to bear, and, if successful, render the British bridgehead over the Jordan useless. In the center stood two elite German battalions and the equivalent of a third slightly weaker, with considerable artillery support. On their right were two Turkish regiments and one was on their left, the whole amounting to the equivalent of an infantry division against a single brigade of light horse. Two of the Turkish regiments had won great distinction in the Jordan Valley in May during the second Trans-Jordan raid, capturing nine British guns of the 4th Australian Light Horse Brigade, the only guns lost in all the campaigns.

The first alarm came in the small hours of July 14, and an artillery barrage was called for in front of the post affected. Some time later the Australians realized what they were in for when they heard orders shouted in German. An hour afterward the enemy poured down the gorge east of the height of Abu Tulul and over the site of a regimental headquarters, which the commanding officer had abandoned just in the nick of time. One troop withdrew after the Germans had swept past; the others clung on, either bypassed or encircled. Then came an attack by the left-hand Turkish regiment which likewise secured a single post, quickly retaken; but the regiments of the right were pinned to the ground.

However, the gallant Germans, filtering through the narrowest of gaps, had made a breach through which they advanced about a thousand yards in a southeasterly direction. They next wheeled northeast to roll up the Australian right flank and advanced about the same distance. Though the fighting had been close and fierce at a single point and the fire heavy on the whole of the narrow front, it does not appear that the German losses had as yet been heavy.

Such reserves as were available for the moment, two squadrons only, were hurried forward by the Australian brigade commander, and one of them, at the point of the bayonet, drove the Germans off their sole holding on the Abu Tulul spur. The enemy still held the height won by his north-eastern drive and clung to it with unequaled courage. The Australians displayed equal courage in their counterattack, but they did not retake it, with a haul of over one hundred prisoners, until 8 A.M. The outposts of the Turkish right were also roughly handled. By now these troops had fallen into confusion and were running about in all directions, delighted to give themselves up if summoned.

It was not only the Turks who had had enough. On hearing that a large party of Germans had installed themselves close to an Australian post, an officer's patrol, fifteen strong, crawled out to reconnoiter. The enemy was found to be some 150 strong, and the little party, almost surrounded, was driven back headlong. Two hours later the same officer crept out again, this time with 20 men, and effected a complete surprise. The enemy fled in disorder to his trenches, leaving 26 prisoners and a machine gun.[9]

The total haul was 448 prisoners, of whom 337 were German. It was the first time, and also virtually the last, that any German troops panicked in Palestine, and on this occasion they had a good excuse. They had been let down and deserted by their Turkish allies, who might have helped them to secure a sparkling local success had they but lived up to their best tradition. As it was the Germans were beaten by their own dash and ran into a trap.

The Australians' success was notable even in their annals. Throughout they resisted coolly and shot straight. They lost two posts temporarily and abandoned one, with some outposts, by permission; otherwise not a single post was entered by the enemy. The correctness of the defense tactics of holding posts wired all around and disregarding what happened on the flanks or even in the rear was proved up to the hilt.

Meanwhile the Turks had come into contact with the Australian and New Zealand Mounted Division and the Imperial Service Cavalry Brigade on the Jordan.* Two Indian regiments sent squadrons over and a Yeomanry regiment and two armored cars also crossed the river. The reconnaissance group found itself faced by a force of cavalry, a brigade of two regiments, so that the brigadier asked Major-General Macandrew to allow further troops to cross and attack the Turkish left. The division commander agreed, but added a warning that they must on no account let themselves be cut off from the crossings.

It was now 10:30 A.M. The Senior Special Service Officer led his regiment along a wadi out of sight of the enemy till he was due south of the hostile flank; then, coming under fire as it emerged, the regiment extended and rode north at a gallop. The cavalry on the immediate Turkish flank fled forthwith into the hills, but the charge crashed into a large body and speared a number with the lance. At sight of the charge the other troops also advanced, but only one regiment had time to drive the attack home, spearing some thirty Turks before the remainder took refuge in a patch of impenetrable scrub. One of the Lancer regiments, having taken over 50 prisoners, had suffered 28 casualties, and the Senior Special Service Officer ordered it to withdraw, an action which was therefore imitated by his colleague. This movement left a Yeomanry regiment isolated some two-and-a-half miles from the Jordan. Another Indian regiment, in the bridgehead the same distance north, was therefore ordered to support it. Moving fast, it suffered little from the Turkish guns, but, finding that the Imperial Service Brigade had withdrawn, was ordered to halt.

* Imperial Service regiments were the contingents of the independent Indian Native States. They were commanded by their Indian officers, but had attached, in every case, several British "Special Service Officers." The Senior Special Service Officer was always a picked man, and he was in practice the commander, since he took orders directly from the brigade commander.

A single troop did not receive the message and charged on to the Turkish trench. At 5:30 P.M. a fresh advance induced the enemy to abandon his position and disappear eastward.

Upwards of a hundred Turks were killed, many of them with the lance, and machine guns accounted for most of the rest. Ninety-one were taken prisoner, including the command- ing officer and all the squadron leaders of one regiment. The British killed and wounded numbered eight-one. In front of or actually in the Turkish trench were found the bodies of the troop leader and six men. Red lances and swords bore witness to the courage with which they had sold their lives.

Liman von Sanders was an honest and truthful man. The only explanation therefore for the travesty of the action which appears in his memoirs is that he was deliberately deceived by the reports. He records that one British party galloped back to the bridges in complete confusion and that the captured Turkish regimental commander and his troops "lost touch with the brigade in the darkness and were taken prisoner." In point of fact the Indian Lancer regiment involved had cap- tured all its prisoners within a hour after noon.[10]

Though Liman had been misled by his subordinates con- cerning this action he was fully—all too fully for his peace of mind—informed about the other one, that fought in the hills, because here his reports came directly from his German troops. They informed him how they had been left to their fate and the consequences. It was not till some time after the war that these facts became public property, in one instance with the publication of the war history of the 11th Reserve *Jäger* Battalion, the withdrawal of which from Palestine has been mentioned. The one company left comprised just about the finest body of men in the Yilderim command. It went into action 142 strong and came out numbering 31. The survivors had not, except in a few cases, actively engaged in the fighting; though their job was dangerous enough, for the most part being runners and telephonists.

Liman mourned his compatriots, but the behavior of the Turkish troops was a matter of still greater concern and particularly to the man who had directed their training before the war and led them to victory at Gallipoli. He put it on record that the Turkish human material, especially the Anatolian, was first class. The best could be got out of them, he wrote, by care for the men, improved food, and the systematic creation of calmer, steadier leadership. He went further than most German officers when he asserted that a high proportion of the Arabs could be made good soldiers if firmly but justly handled from the start.[11]

British officers of our time who have trained and commanded formations and units of the Jordan army know this to be true and not brought about by the advance in education, since they prefer the Bedouin to the townsman, except that he is still unfitted for the "learned arms" and armor. For the Germans however, the situation was far more difficult, since the majority of the Arab troops were disaffected. The Turkish failure was a cruel blow. "Nothing had occurred," Liman writes, "to reveal to me so clearly the decline in the Turkish fighting capacity as the events of July 14." The cavalry had behaved no better than the infantry.

The second action, taking place shortly after, was a British raid upon a steep ridge four thousand yards long which lay west of the Nablus road, by far the biggest raid ever carried out in this theater. The main object was to test the newly-arrived Indian battalions, of which the 10th Division, remolded like the other "Indianized" divisions, had nine, having kept only three of its original Irish battalions. Equipment was as lavish as training. In particular the raiders were provided with felt soles, which were nailed to their boots to prevent slipping and to make their advance noiseless, and bamboo ladders to which were affixed rush matting between two thicknesses of netting to cross the enemy's wire. Before the assault signalers crept out and laid telephone lines three-quarters of a mile in advance of their trenches. Luminous boards were prepared to guide the attackers when the time came to withdraw. The whole of the brigade involved was withdrawn twenty miles behind the front for three weeks' training. A heavy concentration of artillery from the next-door division and the XX Corps heavy artillery was put at its disposal.

On the night of August 12 the attack was launched from both flanks, and after the brigade had established itself in sharp fighting an Irish battalion rolled up the front in face of still tougher opposition. The operation was a success, and, though only 239 prisoners were brought in, a considerable number of Turks were killed. The Indian battalions did well.

Liman thought his men had repelled an attack on a frontage of nine miles, having been deceived by a series of little raids carried out by a division on the right of the 10th Division, and was pleased to record that the whole position remained in Turkish hands. He also mentions, however, that the Turkish troops were depressed by the affluence exemplified by the boots. "They themselves," he writes, "often had only rags tied to their feet, or at best wore 'shariks,' that is, hides laced with string. In many cases even the officers had no other footwear."[8]

Allenby was delighted by the outcome of both actions, perhaps as a cavalryman particularly by that fought astride the Jordan. One instance that came to his notice concerned a single junior officer. Risaldar Shaitan Singh, well mounted, drew right away from his troop and galloped alone straight into the enemy. Before his men rejoined him he had shot two men with his revolver and knocked three more out of their saddles with a loaded stick.

It was this decline in the Turks rather than the disparity in numbers which led a British officer to write after the war —exaggerating for effect—that the final British offensive had been that of "a tiger against a tomcat."

PLANS AND PREPARATIONS

3 THE PLAN which Allenby had been working out in silence and which he did not convey to his corps commanders until August 1 was essentially simple. He would mass the greater proportion of his infantry divisions, five out of seven, and his heavy artillery in the coast plain on a front of no more than eight miles and attack by wheeling forward his left, exactly as a door is opened. Through the doorway all his mounted troops, less the division in the Jordan Valley, would ride fast to cut the Turkish rail communications. In the hills Chetwode's XX Corps, left with only two divisions, could carry out a subsidiary action astride the Nablus road. The most vital objective on the railways was Dera Station, the junction of the Hejaz Railway with the Palestine network, but since he could not reach it in time he proposed to hand it over to Feisal and Lawrence. The left wing was to advance as far as Tul Karm and the Desert Mounted Corps to Sebustiye, supported by a division of the XXI Corps as soon as possible. Then the Desert Mounted Corps was to exploit the success, one division blocking the roads into Nablus and the other two advancing on Haifa.

It was a sound scheme enough, but not a bold one, and it would not have led to the destruction of the Turkish armies.

He thought about it for another three weeks before, on returning from a morning ride, he astonished the corps commanders by an emendation of the most drastic kind. In the first place the XXI Corps was now to take over the task, formerly allotted to the Desert Mounted Corps, of continuing the advance to Sebustiye and Nablus. But it was the role of the cavalry which was most thoroughly transformed. It was to march on El Affule, 25 miles northeast of Tul Karm, and thence enter the Plain of Esdraelon at Lajjun (Megiddo). Dropping forces to close the Turkish retreat northward and northwestward, it was to descend to the Jordan Valley at Beisan.

This was quite another plan, daring, grandiose. If anyone asks whether it was the commander-in-chief's own scheme, let him be answered by another question. What staff officer would put up such a plan, involving the certainty that the cavalry would run away from its transport and have to live on the country, a country which, as has been pointed out, was thought to be more barren than was in fact the case? This plan envisaged throwing a net round the whole hostile force except that part of it which was to be looked after by Major-General E. W. C. Chaytor in the Jordan Valley and on the Hejaz Railway at Amman. It had indeed little relation to the first plan, any more than to the one, frankly pedestrian, put forward by General Smuts after a visit to Allenby and actually approved by the War Office in the spring. Allenby's first scheme was "that of our old friend, *le bon général ordinaire.*"[1]

Here it must be mentioned that Allenby had another visitor shortly after his arrival, in the person of his wife and in tragic circumstances. Their only child Michael had been mortally wounded in France. Allenby was so overcome that the War Office gave her leave to go out, with some reluctance because no one else had such a privilege in time of war in the Middle East. The only sons of generals represent a problem. Two of the war's greatest soldiers, Foch and Franchet d'Espèrey, lost theirs. Foch was outwardly unmoved after the first few minutes, but d'Espèrey declared that he had lost all interest in life. We must wonder if the War Office knew how far Lady Allenby strayed from Cairo. After the war this writer attended a memorial dinner in London in his capacity as historian and heard Allenby's speech, in which he mentioned that he had taken her up into an observation post within easy range of the Turkish artillery.

"It was a hot day and the first thing she did was to put up a white parasol," he said. Then, with a slight smile, he added in his gruff voice: "I soon had that taken down."

The artillery concentration in the plain was very heavy for an outer theater. Bulfin's XXI Corps had at its disposal five 60-pounders and thirteen siege batteries besides the artillery of the infantry divisions, the French detachment, captured Turkish guns, and seven Royal Horse Artillery batteries till called on by the cavalry divisions. It must be noted that the four- or six-gun "battery" of those days is now in the British Army called a "troop," a name used in older days which had temporarily disappeared; also that certain guns and howitzers then described as heavy are now classed as medium. There was no "heavy" machine gun as known today, and the so-called heavy gun was the standard .303 Vickers.

The total amounted to 384 guns and howitzers, whereas the Turkish and German artillery on the same front was estimated at 113, well under a third. It is true that the British had only one gun to each fifty yards as compared to one in ten in contemporary offensives in France, but conditions differed greatly.[2] Ammunition at railheads or in front of them was 1,000 rounds per 18-pdr. field gun and only slightly less for the heavier 60-pdr. guns and 6-in. howitzers. The assault was also to be supported by the destroyers *Druid* and *Forester*.

In quality and range there was no great difference between the artillery of the opposing sides. The German artillery was first class and had been considerably strengthened since Murray's two Battles of Gaza; their Turkish allies had a considerable number of German guns, but with a small proportion of older patterns, the figure for which is unknown. British gunners ranked the German 77-mm. field gun as slightly inferior to their own 18-pounder, but the infantry, which had to face its barrages, rated it very highly. What was known as the *effective* range of the 18-pounder was roughly 5,300 yards, and the maximum rate of *sustained* fire was eight rounds a minute, but both these figures could be largely increased in an emergency. The effective range of the 4.5-in. field howitzer was similar, but the sustained rate of fire only four rounds a minute. The Turks, having been trained by a German mission and rearmed by Germany, used the machine gun developed on the Maxim principle, but their skill in its handling was markedly inferior to that of their allies.

The artillery preparations represented no great problem, apart from hard work and the necessity for concealment. It was otherwise with the movement of ammunition and supplies, which represented one long headache for Major-General Campbell, certainly so far as the cavalry was concerned. These troops were furnished with the day's ration, the iron ration of canned meat and biscuits, and two days' emergency rations carried on the horse and in the limbered wagons. Most of the mounted men, especially the highly paid Australians, also carried luxuries bought in the canteen. A fourth day's ration was to be carried in the divisional trains, and a fifth by a camel convoy. The question mark was, however, how much of all this could keep up. The difficulties emerge if we glance at the allotment of trucks—less than six hundred all told. The XX Corps with two divisions had as many for ammunition as did the XXI Corps with five divisions, and for supplies two-thirds as many. This was solely because the only good north-south road in the country, that from Jerusalem to Nablus and on, was at its disposal. In compensation the XXI Corps got nearly all the camel companies. Chaytor's force in the Jordan Valley had only a trifling amount of transport, including three hundred asses, a traditional means of transportation in Palestine.

Difficulties of communication were almost as great. It must be realized that wireless was still in its early days and apt to be capricious, though much improved since the outbreak of the war, and that portable sets did not exist. The divisions were instructed to establish stations whenever possible, but heavy reliance had to be placed on telephone lines; pigeons were a necessity; and even the heliograph was used. The Director of Army Signals had marked down all the Turkish telegraph and telephone posts, civil as well as military, and issued instructions that they were to be used when possible to save time as well as British cable.

Bridging was also of primary importance, despite the probability that by the sheer speed of the advance some bridges would be secured before the enemy could cut them. Extra bridges had to be thrown across the Nahr el Auja. All of them, but two pontoon bridges, being constructed of heavy imported piles. These, however, aroused no suspicion because there was a bridging school on the river and some of the bridges built by it had been dismantled soon after erection. There was no ruse involved here, the school having been set up before the plan of campaign was tackled, but there could have been no better means of deceiving the enemy. A trestle bridge was to be carried forward and the pontoon park was to throw one trestle over the Nahr Iskanderune, twelve miles north of the front. No other bridging preparations were worth while; if further bridges were called for, they could be sent up and assembled sometime after the advance, but it was impossible to send more on its heels.

The Royal Air Force had a corps wing headquarters at Ramle and allotted a squadron to each corps; one of them being booked to use the Turkish airfield at Jenin as soon as it was taken. Headquarters of the army wing were also established at Ramle. Mention has been made of the Bristol fighters as particularly designed for aggression. There were also two squadrons of single-seater Nieuports with a good reputation as fighters, but their primary role was to cover the bombers. They proved invaluable as an "an express reconnaissance service."[3] Salmond and Borton refused to permit any bombing prior to the attack, except in support of the Arabs.

Before the offensive against the Gaza–Beersheba line in September 1917, Allenby had sanctioned a ruse by his Political Officer, Colonel Richard Meinertzhagen—incidentally his only superior as an ornithologist in the theater; in fact one of the best this country has produced in recent times. Colonel Meinertzhagen, carrying a bunch of documents, rode out into the vast no man's land at a point where it was measured by miles. Turkish cavalry outposts were quickly attracted to the scene, and he let them approach nearer than was comfortable before he turned away. He then pricked his horse and smeared its blood on the papers. Next he played the lame duck, rolling in the saddle as though he had been hit by their fire, while inconspicuously dropping the packet of bloodstained papers. He did not canter off to safety until he had seen the papers picked up. The portfolio was most ingeniously compiled. It contained highly personal letters, a map with arrows pointing at Gaza, an appreciation by an officer lamenting the command's obstinacy in attacking at Gaza rather than Beersheba, and—a pretty touch—a sum of money in notes substantial enough to make it appear that the owner would not willingly lose it. This exploit was without shadow of doubt a factor in inducing the Turkish command to believe that the attack would come at Gaza rather than at Beersheba and thus making its dispositions accordingly.

Nothing equal in ingenuity was effected before the present offensive, but the sum total of the ruses was even more successful. Before, some Turkish officers had their suspicions; this time they were at one in believing that Allenby had his eyes directed over the Jordan to Amman. As already stated, the maintenance of the Australians in the hell of the Jordan Valley was a ruse; how successful, Liman's assignment of his best troops to the offensive at Abu Tulul had proved. It was one of the best, though certain of the other ruses catch the eye more decisively. The principal Jerusalem hotel was taken over hurriedly and its occupants turned out neck and crop; military telephone lines were installed and the various offices marked by cards on the doors. In the region of the city, billets were labeled and a story was spread that a great concentration was to follow. Wireless messages purporting to be from the head-quarters of the Desert Mounted Corps were sent out long after it had moved to the opposite flank. New camps were pitched in the Jordan Valley and some unfortunate troops had to march up and down like a stage army, to raise clouds of dust. Thousands of dummy horses filled the abandoned horse lines. A race meeting was announced for the day on which the offensive was to be opened. And all over the Arab lands Lawrence and his agents spread news that vast quantities of forage would soon be bought and consigned to Amman.[4] It was now an advantage that the front was not continuous and that spies could always bring information to the Turks. The Turkish command was almost completely deceived. Later, captured maps showed only one division of the three of the Desert Mounted Corps as having moved to the coast.

The water problem has been left until last because it was crucial and far more baffling than that of food and ammunition. Seven thousand camels were available to carry water—but at their own pace. Before the start the division on the coast had dug eighty wells. The records of the Palestine Exploration Society were searched for evidence that water had been plentiful in ancient days in places now parched. Allenby himself, who studied avidly every major historical work on Palestine, must have been responsible for this research. The infantry supply was a relatively easy task, and the XXI Corps had in front of it the clean and abundant waters of the Nahr el Auja, which never dried, but it was allotted 2,200 camels of the Camel Transport Corps carrying some 44,000 gallons. Chaytor's force had little to worry about, since the Jordan water, though muddy, is potable. The Desert Mounted Corps had to be furnished with a considerable number of engines and pumps. It started from an ideal position because the Jaffa orange groves could be maintained only by abundant irrigation and were admirably equipped by the prewar Jewish colonies.

These brief particulars afford little notion of the difficulties. The pumping equipment was a regimental issue. Suppose that a detached squadron reached at nightfall a camping ground with a single well as much as two hundred feet deep. Then a canvas bucket had to be lowered on a length of telephone wire, and it would take all night to water the squadron.[5]

The final concentration of the Desert Mounted Corps had been a matter which disquieted its commander, General Chauvel, and which in his view was not entirely righted up to the last. At a conference at GHQ as late as September 11, Bulfin had demanded of Allenby a ruling that the cavalry should not cross the line of his artillery wagons until his artillery had moved forward, which would naturally be a considerable time after the launching of the assault. He was determined that in the event of a big Turkish counterattack, unlikely though this might be, the cavalry should not mask his guns. It is not on record whether Barrow was present, but if not, the corps commander knew his views—Macandrew was hardly concerned, because the 5th Cavalry Division was to ride along the beach. Barrow was only too well aware, from experience in France which Chauvel lacked, how fleeting were the opportunities of cavalry. He did not want to take part in another Cambrai, where the cavalry corps of five cavalry divisions had been blocked and the delay had been appalling.

Solvitur ambulando, or "work it by walking." Neither side was unreasonable, so a compromise was reached. It was arranged that Barrow himself, or a staff officer of his division, should be at the headquarters of the 7th Indian Division, whose commander would inform him at the earliest possible moment that the front was clear enough for the cavalry to go through. It was not all that Barrow desired, but as matters turned out there was no hitch at the start.

The accepted military practice is to give the order of battle and describe the operations from right to left. In this case, however, it will be abandoned, since the whole weight was on the left wing. The XXI Corps operations will be described first and those of its divisions from left to right. Its front ran: 60th, 7th Indian, 75th, 3rd Indian, and 54th Divisions. As previously explained, the 60th and 75th were just as much "Indian" as the 3rd and 7th which had come from Mesopotamia. The only completely English division in the Egyptian Expeditionary Force was the 54th. The right flank was held by the *Détachement Français de Palestine et Syrie*, consisting of two regiments with their own artillery. The two battalions of one of these regiments were Armenians, their nucleus being a large party of refugees, including women and children, who had been rescued by the French navy in August 1915 after a stout defense during the terrible massacres perpetrated by the Turks in that year. The Armenians had, to begin with, plagued Sir John Maxwell by refusing to wash their bodies or clean their camps. Also, they were insubordinate and unwilling to take part in any enterprise. Later, however, a French military mission had induced all the able-bodied men to enlist and had made of them fairly good troops.[6] The other regiment, two battalions of Algerian Tirailleurs, was excellent.

Chauvel, commanding the Desert Mounted Corps, was rather a light-horse leader than a cavalryman, but the Australians of Hodgson's and Chaytor's divisions trusted and admired him. He gave them a free hand within the compass of their orders and did not interfere unnecessarily. The Indian and Yeomanry regiments did not, however, rank him with Major-General Sir George Barrow and Major-General H. J. Macandrew.

When Allenby had had troops enough to form another corps, he had chosen Barrow to command it, but the depleting of the Egyptian Expeditionary Force for reinforcements in France had caused the headquarters to be broken up almost immediately. A small man, as entertaining as he was talkative, Barrow had behind him much experience, including the command of an infantry division in France, and must rank among the best cavalrymen of the war. Macandrew lacked his patience and philosophical temperament, fretted over delays and, as will be related, was to send Allenby a message bordering on the insubordinate—but which, in fact, delighted the commander-in-chief. Macandrew was a first-class thruster. Major-General H. W. Hodgson of the Australian Mounted Division, the last

Englishman to command Australian troops in any theater, was a more cautious type, but had longer experience of the country than either of the others and was trusted by Allenby to meet any emergency. The Australian official historian says of him that he was not an inspired soldier but was sound on conventional lines and possessed of "a sympathetic and engaging personality which went far to make him acceptable to the light horsemen," but hints strongly that they would have preferred an Australian.[7]

Bulfin was almost a stage Irishman. A loyal and patriotic soldier, he yet refused after the war the appointment of commander-in-chief in Ireland because it was wracked by revolt. Had he been in command he would have shot down his fellow countrymen if necessary, but he did not choose to accept such a task. The only thing that upset him was Allenby's obvious preference for Chetwode, a more outstanding character. "Ah, it was always Philup this an' Philup that, an' Philup th' other." Bulfin consoled himself with the reflection that when "Philup" got stuck in the Third Battle of Gaza, Allenby had turned to him, given him the leading role, and for a time immobilized the XX Corps by handing over to him a large proportion of its transport; and that, in the present offensive, Chetwode was left to demonstrate with two divisions in the Judaean hills. Bulfin, as corps commander, lived up to the reputation he had won as a brigadier early in France and Belgium. On the eve of the assault he circulated the message: "Time is the enemy, not the Turks," as the watchword which he demanded every man, including the Indians, should learn.

The commanders of the infantry divisions were not, on the average, up to the standard of Barrow and Macandrew, but two merit a few words of description. Major-General S. M. Shea, commanding the 60th Division, was about the best, but an extraordinarily melodramatic character. Afterwards, in retirement, an enthusiastic Boy Scout and one of Baden Powell's senior lieutenants, he was to be seen in old age tottering to his London club in Scout uniform, including short shorts and wide-awake hat, heedless of the amusement he created. Major-

General A. R. Hoskins, commanding the 3rd Indian Division, was a fine soldier who had been unlucky. On the departure of General Smuts from East Africa he had been appointed his successor and had actually taken over command. However, perhaps at the request of Smuts in London, it was thought wiser to appoint a South African; so Hoskins had to hand over to Major-General J. L. van Deventer, who, it may be added, conducted the rest of the campaign in that theater admirably.

In the Judaean hills Chetwode had decided that an advance on Nablus with only two divisions must be made from the flanks—one division moving along the watershed, the other following parallel spurs with no deep gullies to cross, while a seven-mile gap in the center was to be watched rather than held by a skeleton force. If sufficient speed could be achieved these tactics held out good prospects of capturing the artillery facing the gap. A preliminary wheel on the right was, however, to be made the previous night, September 18, to secure a supply of water in a wadi and enable a track to be driven up one of its tributaries. This would also have the advantage of disquieting the enemy in this quarter and further diverting his attention from the coast plain.

Chetwode's future was to be more outstanding than that of any other of Allenby's subordinates: he became a field-marshal and a peer, and as commander-in-chief in India carried out a radical and much needed reorganization of its army. He had inherited a baronetcy and was universally known as "the Bart." Slight and dapper, drawling through his nose, generally with a cigarette in a long amber holder, he was a combination of energy and imperturbable calm. One of his brigadiers remarked that he felt sure all would go well when the Bart appeared at his headquarters. Superficially, Chetwode was all that Americans most dislike in Britons and that many Britons dislike in their own countrymen, but he was highly capable and, above all, inspired confidence.

The backbone of Chaytor's force in the Jordan Valley was the Australian and New Zealand Mounted Division, the commander of which commanded the whole force. Many of the men were veterans of the Gallipoli campaign where the immortal name "Anzac" had been forged, and they constituted perhaps the most famous troops in their present theater. Described in the first chapter as "gaunt ghosts," none could have been fitter to carry out an operation such as that now planned, provided it could be shortly concluded. The infantry consisted of an Indian brigade, three out of the four battalions of which were Imperial Service, like the cavalry of which there has been mention, and four independent battalions grouped under its orders or those of the force as convenient. Two of these battalions belonged to the British West Indies Regiment, the others being Jewish, formed just before the Balfour Declaration but with it in view. The general expectation was that the West Indians would have but a limited value in attack, whereas the Jews, fighting on the soil of their race, would, though not highly trained, prove ardent and daring. The contrary proved to be the case. The West Indians did all demanded of them and more. The Jews were disappointing and would cause their successors, the brilliant army of Israel, to blush.

"Chaytor was a mounted-infantryman of the highest order, one of those rare soldiers who did everything in this prolonged campaign so surely, thoroughly, and yet so quietly that it might be said no task set him between the Canal and Amman was big enough to test his full capacity."[8]

The Turkish Eighth Army, with headquarters at Tul Karm, held the front from the sea to about twenty miles inland: XXII Corps with two divisions in line and one in reserve on the right; Asia Corps with two divisions in line and the German Brigade in reserve on the left. The army commander was General Jevad Pasha, the successor to Kress von Kressenstein. He was, so far as British information went, outshone by the XXII Corps commander, Colonel Refet Bey. It need hardly be said that Colonel von Oppen, commanding the Asia Corps, was also an exceptional leader, since the German officers had been carefully picked.

The Turkish left flank up to the Jordan consisted of the

Seventh Army—III Corps of 1st and 11th Divisions and the XX Corps of the 26th, 53rd and 24th Divisions. It is needless to describe the army commander, the fiery Mustapha Kemal, but in Colonel Ismet Bey, commanding the III Corps, the reader probably will not recognize a great figure of the later war with Greece and a great president of the Turkish Republic, Ismet Pasha Inönnü. The XX Corps was commanded by Major-General Ali Fuad Pasha. The only reserves under Liman's hand were three regiments, whereof two were depot regiments.

Beyond the Jordan was the Fourth Army, of which only one corps and army troops were in contact with the British. This was the VIII Corps, of the 48th and Composite Divisions, the Caucasus Cavalry Brigade, which had behaved so badly at the Jordan fords, and a few heterogeneous battalions. The army troops, weak 3rd Cavalry Division and superb German 146th Regiment, constituted the best part of this corps. The remainder of the Fourth Army was widely spread, with a division at Amman and a strong detachment in the region of Ma'an.

The Fourth Army commander, Mohammed Jemal Pasha the Lesser, was for the time being the best Turkish soldier in this theater of war, since Mustapha Kemal was in one of his sulky and irresponsible moods, almost demented by his hatred of the Germans. Unlike many otherwise good Turkish leaders, Jemal was quick on his feet. He was skilled in maneuver and resolute, and, writing later, Liman goes out of his way to praise him.

Allenby's chief of staff, Major-General Sir L. J. Bols, had served in the same capacity in France and one of Allenby's first actions had been to demand that this cheerful friend and companion should be sent out. The main weight of the operations staff work was, however, borne by Brigadier-General W. H. Bartholomew, who had earlier headed Chetwode's staff. The calmest and most equably-minded of men, "Barty" suffered from one nightmare. If, he confided to T. E. Lawrence, the Turks should withdraw a distance of seven or eight miles in the coast sector, this would save their army and leave the British "like a fish flapping on dry land".[9]

Liman was given one sensational warning. An Indian sergeant deserted on September 17 and disclosed that the attack would come in the coast plain. Liman had a dangerously short time in which to act, but he had no intention of withdrawing, despite the fact that the army and corps commanders, Jevad and Refet, had for some time been imploring him to do so. He has been much blamed on this account, and it is often said that he believed the deserter to have been planted on him. Perhaps we should say "suspected" rather than "believed." A profound student of Turkey in the First World War, the Frenchman, Commandant Larcher, has made three points not brought out in British or German accounts. First, supposing the deserter told the truth, the Indian sergeant did not know that it would be the *main* attack, and Liman hoped that, if it were not, he would be able to hold with a moderate loss of ground. Secondly, if it were, Liman would not know the direction and supposed it would be on Nablus, unaware that the cavalry was posted to strike nearly due northward. Thirdly, a quick withdrawal with guns and baggage would have been difficult and hazardous because the two armies west of Jordan had at their backs, in the Samarian and Judaean hills respectively, narrow defiles, to say nothing of, beyond them, a single-track railway through El Affule, Beisan, and Dera towards Damascus.[10] The commander-in-chief probably did the right thing in the circumstances, but there can be no doubt that his decision to cancel the strategy bequeathed to him by Falkenhayn was a long step toward the destruction of his forces now impending.

What Allenby thought is unknown. He kept no diary and wrote nothing in later life about the war. His comments on the draft history submitted to him amounted to a dozen brief sentences, one of which referred in eight words to an incident in the second Trans-Jordan operation: "Then I got wrong information at Corps (Chauvel's) H.Q."; a second gave

Hodgson a word of praise; the rest were confined to grammar, on which he was most punctilious. We may be sure he remained unperturbed. If there is fussing, it is the staff officer who should do it and the commander-in-chief who should be serene.

BULFIN OPENS THE GATE; CHETWODE MANEUVERS IN THE HILLS

4 PALESTINE EXPERIENCES sweltering days in autumn, even on the coast when there is no sea breeze. September 18 was one such day and highly oppressive. Even when darkness cooled the air there was for some but small relief. Senior officers and the more thoughtful juniors who had been asking whether Johnny Turk would go were now asking whether Johnny Turk was gone. Few believed that a Turkish withdrawal would nullify hopes of a striking success, even if the position proved to be held only by machine guns and skirmishers. In that case it seemed certain that the enemy would be in some measure disorganized, but they felt that their problem would be far stiffer and the haul of prisoners much smaller.

Bartholomew had exaggerated when he foretold that in the event of a withdrawal the British would be left like a fish out of water, but they *would* face a serious setback. Their leaders had to ask themselves how much the deserter had known and to what extent he had been believed. There were some doubts whether the training of a number of Indian battalions was adequate. A partial success would not be good enough. But when the British bombardment opened with a tremendous crash at 4:30 A.M., then, and only then, were the most anxious minds set at rest by the hundreds of signal rockets which soared into the air from the Turkish trenches.

Shea's 6oth Division on the coast had been formerly in the Judaean hills, but after relief had been given a week's hard training. It was in origin a very fine London division, and though it had lost nine battalions of the London Regiment, at least four of the Indian replacements—three of Punjabis and the famous 2nd Guides—were excellent. To reach its objective the division had the longest distance to cover, fourteen miles as the crow flies and sixteen by the route it had to follow. Its first task was to establish a bridgehead over a stream for the passage of the 5th Cavalry Division along the coast; its second task was to capture Tul Karm. It was to fight upon a historic battlefield. Between Arsuf and the Nahr el Faliq—also on a baking September day—there had been decided one of the greatest and fiercest encounters of the Crusades when Richard Coeur de Lion, against enormous odds, defeated Saladin and avenged the disaster of Hattin.[1]

The assault of the left brigade, the 180th, commanded by Brigadier-General C. F. Watson—he had fought well at Third Gaza and distinguished himself still more in the capture of Jerusalem—was carried out in two columns, the trusty 2nd Guides flanked by the Mediterranean. The attack was a complete success and the Guides took some 600 prisoners, but the losses were heavy by the standard of that day, numbering 414. The center battalion was ordered to march straight on Tul Karm, flanked by battalions on either side of the road. The 5th Australian Light Horse Brigade had been put at Shea's disposal and he had ordered it not to worry about Tul Karm but to leave the town to the infantry and, instead, cut the road to Nablus. Veering left to avoid the infantry battle, the brigade reached the road soon after noon, pushed along at a good round pace by Brigadier-General G. M. M. Onslow, who had succeeded one of the officers "cast for age" by Allenby after the Third Battle of Gaza. Here a squadron of the French cavalry made a dashing charge on an Austrian battery and took all the guns and men.[2] The little garrison in Tul Karm and the much larger number of fugitives fought stoutly, despite bombing by a flight of British aircraft, which caused a good deal of confusion. The town was, however, taken at 5 P.M. by a battalion of the Londoners with some 800 prisoners, but the lion's share fell to the cavalry. It rounded up the mob streaming northward and captured about 2,000 men, with fifteen guns. The French pursued those who had escaped the net, stayed out all night, and returned on the morrow with several hundred more captives.

The 7th Indian Division was under the command of Major-General Sir V. B. Fane, an Indian Army officer of wide experience, but who, Bulfin thought, inclined to be pigheaded. General Fane was—perhaps for that reason—to breach the enemy's second line of defense, which ran through Et Tire. To start with, the division would be supported by heavy artillery alone—because the field artillery would be limbering up or already on the move—and was therefore ordered not to incur needless loss if resistance should prove too stout, but to halt and await the batteries. On the division's right the 19th Brigade, under the command of a cavalryman, Brigadier-General W. A. Weir, who was to return to his own arm before the campaign was over, had two battalions of the 21st temporarily attached. The brigade got its first objectives easily and was then concerned in two remarkable incidents.

In the first, *Naik* (Corporal) Buta Khan, 92nd Punjabis, lost touch with his battalion but picked up a little party of the 1st Guides. He and four of these were wounded and returned a short distance to be bandaged by a medical orderly. He then went forward again with his wounded following. Suddenly they came in sight of a heavy howitzer battery and saw horses and bullocks being led up to haul it out. The *Naik* immediately placed his men between the guns and teams, went back alone, and from a piece of high ground attracted the attention of a Punjabi company, which promptly captured the battery. It was a remarkable feat of combined intelligence and pluck. Indian sergeants were often capable of a considerable degree of initiative, but it was rare to find a corporal with so much.

The other affair concerned a British officer, Captain T. W. Rees, who with six men captured all but one gun of a field howitzer battery. The fourth gun having been hooked in and driven away, Rees jumped on a captured pony, galloped after it, and forced the drivers to bring it back. Here was indeed a welcome signal of demoralization in the enemy's ranks, and there were soon to be more.

The other brigade, the 21st, with its remaining two battalions captured the foremost system of defense and then pushed through a Gurkha battalion to roll up a section of the front not previously attacked. The whole brigade then concentrated and marched on Et Tire, which had already been captured by the 75th Division. After crossing the Tul Karm road, however, the brigade found matters less easy than at the start and was pinned to the ground by a German battalion. It could make no further move before morning. In the meantime, the reserve brigade, the 28th, followed by a whole artillery brigade, advanced in diamond formation, to find the enemy's rear guard standing on high ground northwest of Et Tire, and quickly forced him back.

The 75th Division, under Major-General P. C. Palin, a sound man but more at home in Indian mountain warfare than in a plain such as this and who was sometimes a little slow, had no distant objective because it was not called on to take part in the wheel. Its task, however, proved difficult, especially that of its right brigade. This brigade was commanded by Brigadier-General H. J. Huddleston, one of the best of his rank in the Egyptian Expeditionary Force and destined to become a distinguished commander-in-chief in the Sudan for a great part of the Second World War after serving as G.O.C. Northern Ireland. The brigade's objective was the defense system of Et Tire and it was supported by the South African Field Artillery Brigade, the only white troops of the Union in the theater. It was soon held up by the Turkish reserve division, the 46th, commanded by the German Major Tiller, who had saved Gaza in the First Battle.* The position was

---

* He would have been a temporary major-general in the British Army, and there were several in France with the substantive rank of major. The Germans were, however, chary on this subject and with them temporary rank was virtually unknown.

finally turned from the right with the aid of armored cars
and a squadron of the Corps Cavalry Regiment. A triumph
followed—the capture of the Turkish XXII Corps headquarters
with all its documents. This was only the beginning of a
process which explains why Turkish records are so scanty. It
was to be repeated on a bigger scale at Nazareth, but here
many of them were destroyed. Thousands of appreciations,
reports, and orders were taken. In most cases, for reasons which
the state of the communications makes clear, the duplicates
had for a long time not been sent to Constantinople. In the
heat of the moment British officers often failed to secure documents which would have been precious to historians. Brigadier-General C. A. H. Maclean's 234th Brigade had an easier
task. Supported by strong and accurate artillery fire, it speedily
secured its objective. Its losses were 578, two-thirds of those in
Huddleston's brigade.

The capture of his headquarters ended the active service
of the Turkish corps commander in this theater, Refet Bey,
who was cut off with his aide-de-camp and two orderlies. For
the better part of a week he sought a way out. So far as is
known he spoke no English, but he moved always by night and
answered challenges by saluting and riding on at a walk. He
finally reached Tyre, 75 miles to the north, but this was after
the capture of Damascus. After Ismet Pasha, he was to be
Mustapha Kemal's best lieutenant against the Greeks in the
Anatolian campaign of 1919–1922.

General Hoskins ordered his 3rd Indian Division to advance, two brigades in line, in the general direction of Qalqilye
and Jaljulye, on the railway south of Et Tire. On the right the
7th Brigade met hardly any resistance in the front-line defenses,
though one battalion suffered nearly a hundred casualties from
artillery before reaching them. Shrapnel would have caused
far more, but of that the Turks had little or none; they were
armed by their German masters who, like the French, were
firm believers in high-explosive. Qalqilye was secured by 9
A.M., but the afternoon orders for a further advance reached
the battalion concerned so late that most of its march was

made in the dark, and it kept going till midnight. The 9th Brigade had better luck with the artillery barrage and gave the Turkish infantry no chance to pull itself together. After the position through Qalqilye had been broken, however, the fact that the 75th Division had not taken part in the wheel caused some trouble; it was to have been squeezed out at this stage, but a gap still existed. Still, the first objective was taken by nightfall. A company of the 8th Brigade now advanced and by about 6 A.M. secured intact a railway bridge over a small wadi west of Qalqilye, a useful piece of work. After a brief but heavy bombardment another battalion took Qalqilye, finding its capture an easy task because the enemy was in a nervous state owing to the pressure of the 7th Brigade on his flank. The advance was resumed in the afternoon, and the brigade did not go into bivouac until last light.

It might be thought that the pivot of the wheel, the 54th Division and the *Détachement Français de Palestine et Syrie* (*D.F.P.S.*), which had been placed under the orders of the divisional commander, Major-General S. W. Hare, had the easiest task, but it proved the stiffest. Hare was no genius, but he conducted the attack competently and was lucky enough to have at his disposal a brilliant brigade commander, Brigadier-General Angus McNeill. The latter, an expert on Arab horses, settled down after the war near Acre and supervised their purchase and training for the Arab Legion in Trans-Jordan. The *D.F.P.S.*, under the command of Colonel P. de Piépape, got its objective quickly, the excellent Algerian Tirailleurs on the left showing dash as well as skill in maneuver. On their left, McNeill directed the assault of his 163rd Brigade on Bidye. In the first phase the Turks launched the only counterattack of the day, and that with a single company. They came on stoutly, but the hot fire of a platoon of Tirailleurs in their flank put most of them out of action and brought about the surrender of the rest. Bidye, however, was not captured until about 3 A.M. on the following day, September 19. Meanwhile the 161st Brigade under Brigadier-General H. B. Orpen-Palmer had at first advanced quickly, but before the final objective was taken

the resistance—strengthened by the right of a German battalion of the Asia Corps which had not been attacked frontally
—had become very determined. It was therefore necessary to
mount a fresh bombardment by the whole divisional artillery,
after which all was plain sailing. The 162nd Brigade, commanded by Brigadier-General A. Mudge, was not required to
concentrate until 8 A.M. or to begin its advance till an hour
later. Its troops became intermixed with those of the 161st,
but the confusion was quickly straightened out. One battalion
kept on the move until the small hours of September 20. The
54th Division and the D.F.P.S. took some 700 prisoners and
nine guns, for a casualty list of 536. These troops were lucky.
In the victorious battles on the western front, divisions were
still suffering losses five or more times greater. There is a far
higher proportion of Palestinian veterans walking about today,
though they may suffer periodically from "the shivers," the
malarial infection that is so hard to eradicate.

The haul of prisoners of the XXI Corps was not as yet
great, but still it exceeded 7,000 prisoners and a hundred guns,
while the remnants of the two Turkish divisions in the coast
plain were nearly all doomed, since the cavalry was about to
block their escape routes. Before the cavalry's exploits are re-
counted, however, the achievement of the British XX Corps
in the Judaean hills must be dealt with and the Turkish reaction more closely studied.

It has already been pointed out that Sir Philip Chetwode
was operating with his two divisions widely separated. They
were also widely extended. This time, since Major-General S.
F. Mott's 53rd Division was opening the attack during the
previous night, we may revert to the practice of describing the
operations of the Battle of Nablus from right to left. The plan
was very different from that in the plain, since both terrain
and resources differed markedly. Success depended mainly on
the progress of the XXI Corps, secondly on the tactical skill of
commanders and the staying power of troops in genuine hill
warfare. There was only one road deserving of the name, that

from Jerusalem which ran down to the Jordan at Beisan, thirty miles ahead, and this could not be used to begin with because it was certain to be strongly defended. Good legs, good wind, and endurance were called for as urgently as courage.

Mott first decided to capture a deep depression, three miles each way, by encircling it with a brigade from either side. On the right the 160th Brigade was to cross the gorge of the Wadi Auja, which ran out of it to the Jordan.* The brigade descended into the gorge at the only point where the drop was not precipitous. As the advanced guard climbed out it came under machine-gun and artillery fire in the moonlight, but by 3 A.M. on September 19 the brigade was well round to the northern side of the basin. Brigadier-General N. E. Money's 159th Brigade did not start until 10:30 P.M., four hours after the 160th. One battalion had some trouble because the only two British officers unwounded spoke no Hindustani, while the Indian officers did not know the plan. The short delay may have influenced adversely the attack on the next objective, which was repulsed after hard fighting by the Turkish 26th Division. However, the last objective, apart from the ridge on which the Turks stood, was taken. The check had, nonetheless, one unhappy effect: the road which was to have been constructed across the depression could not be completed and the artillery was thus held up.

The commander of the 10th Division, Major-General J. R. Longley, had a difficult problem. He wanted to concentrate as close as possible to his front line in order to keep his troops fresh for a long advance, but did not know whether he would have to wait twelve or thirty-six hours. He solved his problem by concentrating well forward and dumping five days' supplies for his men's use, drowning the noise of the trucks with artillery fire. Nevertheless, the division had to be fed for the next two days by pack transport.

At noon on September 19 Chetwode, on Allenby's initia-

---

* Not to be confused with the Nahr el Auja, running into the Mediterranean. "Nahr" means "river"; "wadi" a river bed, dry or nearly so in summer.

tive, ordered General Longley to attack that night. Brigadier-General C. L. Smith's 29th Brigade had to make the first breach, after which the 31st Brigade was to widen it. The assault was launched at 7:45 P.M., but one battalion met such strong resistance that the barrage ran right away from it. However, the barrage was brought back, and then the ridge on which the Turks had been holding out was carried by a bayonet charge. A rocket was fired as a signal for the 31st Brigade, under Brigadier-General E. M. Morris, to assault. The operation was completely successful; the vital road could at last be pushed forward; and the greater part of the divisional artillery could advance to support a further attack. Taking into account the difficulties facing Chetwode's corps, the nature of the ground, and the fact that his two divisions were opposed by four, whereas Bulfin's five divisions faced only three, Chetwode had done very well, and his divisional commanders had fully lived up to his leadership. Bulfin was the bludgeon, Chetwode the master of maneuver. Both roles were necessary in carrying through Allenby's plan. He knew his men and their respective virtues.

The Royal Air Force had prevented the enemy from pulling himself together—above all by bombing, which paralyzed his nerve centers and spread death and destruction behind his front. It also provided invaluable information, which was almost always the first to reach the commander-in-chief. The headquarters of the Turkish Eighth Army at Tul Karm and that of the Seventh at Nablus came under heavy attack. From Tul Karm, Liman, at Nazareth, never had another message; though he got some from Nablus, where the telephone exchange was repaired by noon. Not until then did he partially realize, for the first time, the extent of the disaster. The central exchange was bombed thrice: during the night, in the early morning, and between 10 A.M. and 12 noon. It was the target of the best aircraft, including the lone Handley-Page, and was gravely damaged. Bombing of the roads was begun and the road from Tul Karm to Nablus was more than once blocked

by smashed vehicles and dead horses, but in general the effects
were not nearly so devastating as those which were to follow.[3]
One consequence was that the Turks, whose artillery had had
no particular reason to stack large quantities of shell with the
guns because they were not expecting an attack and did not
want to see dumps blown up by the better provided British
artillery, speedily ran out of ammunition and were unable to
replace it.[4] The RAF also rendered good service by laying
smoke screens on two occasions in front of brigades of the
XXI Corps.

To turn to the tribulations of the Turkish command,
some time after nine o'clock Liman learned from Colonel von
Oppen, commanding the Asia Corps, of which only one German battalion was engaged, that the coast defenses had been
completely breached and that the British cavalry was streaming north through the passes in the Samarian hills. The news
must have come to Liman as a sickening shock, since he had
till now no conception of how great was the disaster. Through
Seventh Army Headquarters he next heard that Oppen, on
his own initiative, had already committed one of his three
German battalions, two Turkish battalions, and a cavalry squadron of both nations to intervention. Meanwhile, the Turkish
19th Division—one of the crack formations of Yilderim which
had served Falkenhayn nobly and balked Allenby north of
Jerusalem—had weakly abandoned its position at Jaljulye before the little town had come under attack. This was another
shock for Liman to find that some of his best troops had so
deteriorated. Oppen sent a German lieutenant with a few
clerks to rally the division, but they succeeded only in part.[5]
The commander-in-chief's sole consolation was that his Seventh
Army was, in general, holding its ground; though the III Corps
was falling back to make a junction with the Asia Corps.
Oppen next ordered back the guns and baggage before shifting his headquarters. His Germans and the 16th Turkish Division fought with great gallantry and stubbornness, abandoning
one position for the next only when this became urgently

necessary.[6] Every order Oppen gave was characterized by tactical skill, boldness, and resolution.

The Seventh Army now reported to Liman that it had beaten off most of the attacks but was about to fall back to its second position, and he could only assent. Though he had received so much bad news, he had still no clear picture of what was happening in the Plain of Sharon and was not to have till the day was out. He believed the XXII Corps to be retiring in fairly good order, whereas it had virtually ceased to exist. The British cavalry had already penetrated deeply.

Before turning to the British cavalry, the further progress of the infantry must be briefly described. The main attack of the 53rd Division had now passed to the fresh 158th Brigade, commanded by Brigadier-General H. A. Vernon. It had started with a dashing bayonet attack by the Cape Corps, South African natives in the 160th Brigade. These men could charge, but had little ability to hold on in adversity. They were driven back with serious loss and, as happens often with impressionable troops, the leaders suffered most, thirteen of the twenty-one white officers in this action being killed or wounded. An Indian battalion now had to repair the damage. The 158th Brigade had been delayed by the eternal business of putting through the artillery road, and after a good start was held up by a stout Turkish rear guard, whereupon Mott ordered the brigade to await darkness. The skeleton force astride the Nablus road now came into action. One section, first-class Yeomanry of the Corps Cavalry Regiment, found the road clear for well over a mile, and then covered only by small rear guards easily ejected. Two pioneer battalions of this force could now be released, so that a through road was soon complete.

The 10th Division of Chetwode's XX Corps found the enemy's new line of defense well organized and strongly held. The right of the 29th Brigade advanced with great determination, meeting dogged resistance from German troops almost from the first, but making steady progress. The 31st Brigade moved two hours later, having been delayed by the final work on the new road. After a fine start the brigade was stopped dead by fire from high ground on which it could not discern the enemy's position because the hills were so heavily wooded. Repeated attempts to storm were stopped by machine-gun fire and cost over 150 men. As soon as two field-artillery brigades could get into action, however, the effort was renewed and a Sikh battalion of the 29th Brigade made a typically dashing attack between the two battalions in the lead. A company of the Royal Irish Fusiliers of the 31st, faced by very tough opposition, was warned by the battalion commander that if the men ran fast they might not be killed but if they were slow they would be. The company took the position with the bayonet: suffering but slight loss.

Chetwode, a young man for his rank, had been personally active, seeing as much as possible with his own eyes. He could not, however, have gained and maintained so tight a grip on the situation if he had not, before and during the battle, impressed on his subordinates the extreme importance of quick and accurate information regarding both the enemy and his own troops, more vital and more difficult to obtain in the hills than in the plain. This had always been an outstanding feature of the training before the battle, and one which—as a cavalryman active in command of troops of his own arm in the open warfare of the early stages in France and under Murray in the advance into Palestine—he thoroughly understood.

Chetwode now had in front of him three passages down to the Jordan Valley, but by far the most important was that which followed the Wadi Fara. Though the country looked uninviting and it was easy enough to lose the way, he urged the 53rd Division to continue the advance after dusk. Major-General Mott thereupon directed the 158th and 159th Brigades —which now reversed their position with the 10th Division— to cut the first route. Here there was no resistance, the Turks having withdrawn as Chetwode had foreseen. Chetwode had now displayed another virtue, his ability to penetrate the mind of his foe, one of the most valuable gifts of a commander. He was well seconded by the heavyweight hunting man Mott, who rode forward on one of his big horses, well known in point-to-point races at home, to a report center established just behind the front, and directed the two brigade commanders to press on at their best speed. Mott got a fine response from tired men. By the evening of September 21 a battalion of the 158th Brigade had covered ten miles from its position of the day before. However, the corps commander at this stage ordered the division to halt. Its task was done and there was now no need to press on to the Wadi Fara. The division had taken 2,000 prisoners at a cost of 690 killed, wounded, and missing.

It was the British air arm that had saved these men, who by this time could hardly put one foot before the other, from further exertions. Early that morning the planes had begun a devastating attack on the Turkish artillery and transport as the jaded horses made their way painfully down the winding road toward the Jordan. The leading role was played by the Bristol fighters of the Australian Royal Air Force, the best two-seaters in the theater, with a speed of over 100 miles an hour. (If this sounds absurdly low to modern ears, it must be realized that the maximum speed of the aircraft in use at the beginning of the war was between sixty and seventy miles an hour.) The single-seater S.E.5s, fractionally faster but capable of carrying only light bombs, also played a part.[7] It became clear before evening from the pilots' reports that the road was blocked, but not until it had been examined next morning at close quarters could the damage be assessed. One of the best word pictures of the chaos on the road was painted by a Signals officer, who had no reason to make it worse than it was because his sole purpose had been, as he put it after the war, "to loot telephone wire."

Over 100 guns, 55 trucks, and 92 country carts were found in complete confusion.[8] Ammunition, stores, and food were spilled all over the place. Yet the actual damage done by bombs was small, in the Signals officer's eyes unexpectedly so until he realized that the bombers could not hit a road running along the flank of a ravine. There was, in fact, hardly any sign of a direct hit and very few dead men, while the Turks had been able to carry their wounded with them. Yet the attack can still fairly be described as devastating because its moral effect had been so overwhelming and had evidently caused a panic. An air photograph published in the official history of the campaign covering a section of the strung-out Turkish retreat shows only a single dead horse, but the observer mentioned and others reported that they were more numerous than men. What had happened in one case was that truck drivers had jumped out, leaving their engines running; the trucks had then run into the tail of artillery in front; the guns in their turn had been carried into transport wagons; and finally an accumulation of dead horses and smashed material had brought the avalanche to a halt. It took the British several days to extricate the guns, and most of the carts were simply burnt.

Nothing of the kind was accomplished by aircraft during the contemporary retreat of the Germans on the western front because there were no similar defiles, though the number of aircraft engaged was infinitely greater. The sole parallel is to be found in the attacks on Bulgarian transport in a pass east of the Vardar in Macedonia after the great Allied victory, and there also moral effect played a great part.

The 10th Division resumed its advance on the night of September 20 shortly before midnight. The big final effort demanded of it was to secure Nablus, and the hardest task was allotted to Brigadier-General F. A. Greer, whose 30th Brigade was already weary after hard work on the road. It passed through the 29th Brigade and reached the Damascus road a few miles north of Nablus at 5:20 P.M., up to which time no man in its battalions had enjoyed more than six hours' sleep in forty-eight. That day Allenby visited the brigade. He drove up to the Irish and Indian battalions in the lead and urged them to keep going despite their exhaustion. It was a remarkable example of moral influence and also of the truth of the old adage quoted in many armies: that sweat saves blood. The work of the XX Corps was now all but over.

It may here be mentioned that Allenby removed one of the brigadiers of the 53rd Division as slack and disobedient. Owing to Allenby's explosive temper the impression got about that he was ruthless to subordinates and "a dealer in bowler hats," the traditional London headgear of the officer in plain clothes. But this was not the case. He had relieved very few regimental or battalion commanders, and then generally because they appeared to him rather too old for their jobs in a theater which demanded high physical fitness. He had sent home an infantry brigadier who was considered to have mishandled the passage of the Nahr el Auja—incidentally, this headstrong and hard-fighting man had, under Murray, caused some confusion at First Gaza by leading his brigade to a position he liked the look of better than the one allotted to him and then being lost in the fog for a considerable time. Allenby was also to dismiss two outstanding cavalry brigadiers in circumstances to be recorded, but the total number of victims was not excessive. Allenby's temperament was one not altogether rare, especially in soldiers. No one close to him doubted that he was well aware of the unfairness which swept over him in his passionate moments. He never apologized for them openly, but he did so by friendliness and kindness. His staff officers in particular found him a delightful companion, who could talk politics nearly as well as birds and flowers. The best evidence of this comes not from Palestine but from the late General Sir Charles Grant, the second string to General Bols on the operations staff in the Battle of Arras, who had vivid recollections of Allenby's agreeable small talk during evening walks after business.

In the XXI Corps Bulfin issued orders for the continuance of the advance early on September 20 by the four divisions remaining after the withdrawal of the 75th. The 5th Light

Horse Brigade was ordered to start at 2 A.M. from Tul Karm and cut the railway north of Sebustiye, afterwards making for Jenin. Brigadier-General Onslow moved up the Vale of Barley, picking up a light armored-car battery. However, having bypassed Nablus with his Australian regiments while the French cavalry entered the town and found it evacuated, his troops became so strung out that it was impossible to reach Sebustiye in daylight. Onslow was therefore ordered to rejoin the Australian Mounted Division, and his detachment came to an end with the capture of over 8,000 prisoners.[9]

On the right the 54th Division had virtually nothing to do. The 3rd Indian Division, on the other hand, had plenty, coming at once in contact with stouthearted and skilful German troops. The division had no artillery with which to budge them because the 19th Mountain Brigade of the Corps Artillery, with its pack guns and howitzers, had been attached to the 8th Brigade. The result was temporary deadlock. Major-General Hoskins, fuming over the delay, rode forward to see the situation for himself and sent a message to the 428th Battery of the Divisional Artillery that it *must* push forward a single howitzer, which it did. Since even its lofted fire failed to clear a high ridge at the requisite range, the battery pushed on boldly over high ground, completely exposed, to short range and came into action again. The movement acted like a charm and the enemy disappeared. The 7th Brigade reached Oppen's abandoned headquarters and the camp of his reserve, capturing much useful foods and stores. Another battalion bit into his retreat, the first time this wily man had been caught. The 1st Connaught Rangers came down on a column of artillery, taking five guns and many horses and vehicles. The 9th Brigade was delayed rather by raging thirst than the enemy's resistance, but it had to use the tactics familiar on the Indian North-West Frontier, "crowning the heights" with a series of small parties which remained motionless until the column has passed through so that the track should not be subjected to observed hostile fire—tactics which had not been employed since the advance on Jerusalem. The division reached the point where the short railway line to Nablus branched off from the main line.

The 7th Indian Division advanced in two columns. On the right the 21st Brigade was soon brought to a halt because the troops were prostrated for lack of water, but a number of wells were soon found. Though the 19th Brigade had outdistanced it, this brigade, too, needed water badly, and the only likely source was held by the enemy. Brigadier-General Weir took some little time to decide what to do, but finally attacked at 2 P.M. without awaiting artillery support—withheld because horses and mules need water as much as men. The 1st Seaforth Highlanders was stopped by cactus hedges and there was nothing for it but to await the guns. Only a 3.7-in. mountain howitzer battery arrived, but this sufficed. The village of Beit Lid was cleared by the 28th Punjabis with hand grenades, a method with which the troops in this theater were less familiar than their comrades on the western front. In the 60th Division, Brigadier-General E. T. Humphreys's 179th Brigade, in reserve on September 20, went forward rapidly, driving rear guards off one ridge after another, and securing a railway tunnel in which explosive charges had already been laid for demolition.

Little need be said about the following day, September 21, when the 28th Brigade, after marching all night, took Sebustiye (the Samaria of the Bible) with over 600 prisoners. These troops, like those of the XX Corps, saw in the darkness the dim shades of Bedouin, their camels loaded with Mausers, making for the Jordan Valley and beyond.

The captures cannot be given exactly because the return of prisoners for the whole corps was made up to October 18, but they can be estimated very closely at 12,000, with 149 guns. Up to October 18, the day the 7th Indian Division reached Beirut, the XXI Corps took 12,675 prisoners, together with three engines and fifty-six railway wagons, a number of which were brought into use. The report of Allied losses, compiled on October 22, gave 446 killed, 2,619 wounded, and 313 missing—34 officers (British 23, Indian 11) killed, and 129

officers (British 103, Indian 26) wounded; 414 rank and file
(British 195, Indian 219) killed; and 2,690 (British 876, Indian
1,314) wounded. Three hundred and thirteen men (British 129,
Indian 184) were missing, no British officers coming into this
category.[10] A certain number of wounded in field ambulances
may not have been reported even by the latter part of October.
In this corps the proportionate losses in British rank and file
illustrate the big part played by the British infantry, since its
battalions amounted only to one quarter.

The captures of the XX Corps numbered 6,961 prisoners.
The losses were 1,505: 13 officers (9 British, 4 Indian) killed;
51 officers (32 British, 19 Indian) wounded: 212 rank and file
(60 British, 152 Indian) killed; 1,211 rank and file (222 British,
989 Indian) wounded; 18 rank and file (4 British, 14 Indian)
missing.[11]

On the Turkish side the Eighth Army Commander, Jevad
Pasha, and his subordinate, Colonel von Oppen, were having
a sorry time of it. Jevad, who had opened a new headquarters
at Masudiye Station, strove by every means in his power to
impose some order among the fleeing Turks. During the night
of September 20 Colonel von Oppen received an order which
cannot have come from Jevad and almost certainly came from
Mustapha Kemal—who had no right to issue it—to send over
his troops to cover the retreat of the Seventh Army. Oppen
naturally refused to do so, and would not in any case have had
much to send. Next morning he had to combine two of his three
German battalions into one, and even this consisted only of a
single rifle company and the trench-mortar group. At 10 A.M.
on September 21 Oppen got a report that the upper part of
the Wadi Fara was closed, and thought himself as good as
hemmed in when he learnt that the next passage also was
closed. He extricated himself with superb skill, and that night
contrived to put his Turkish 16th and 19th Divisions into
Tubas, on the road from Nablus to Beisan, unaware that
British cavalry had already reached the Jordan at the latter

place. Apart from guns and baggage, Mustapha Kemal's Seventh Army remnants were in time to march down the Wadi Fara.

The British infantry had fought splendidly. It can be said that there had been hardly an instance of weakness such as is to be found in the records of the most successful campaigns and is not absent from those of the final campaign on the western front. Yet it is only fair to add that the latter was infinitely more arduous and bloody. The Turks, with rare exceptions, failed to live up to their standards in the Gallipoli campaign and in the Caucasus. If the Germans were very much more formidable, they were also better equipped and better fed. A participant on the British side goes so far as to assert that in the retreat from Nablus to Sebustiye some of the German troops did little better than the Turkish. No other eyewitness confirms this criticism, which thus may be safely disregarded, but the Germans did not always behave quite so well in this phase as when Lawrence saw them later on.[12]

It was strong legs as much as courage that won, especially in the Judaean hills. It would not be too much to say that in all the hill fighting the terrain represented 40 per cent of the difficulties to be overcome. If so, the achievement of the Royal Engineers and Army Service Corps must count another 40 per cent. The road-making of the former was as important as their work on water supply, which time after time set troops going again when they seemed to be finished. Horse-mastership has not been mentioned because it was much more remarkable in the cavalry. In any case the endurance of animals pulling field guns and carrying packs is more severely taxed than that of horses pulling horse-artillery guns and carrying men, even when these are festooned with ammunition, food, and other necessities to an extent recalling the practice of Don Quixote. Man's best friend was still his best friend here, if for the last time in war.

THE CAVALRY FINDS THE
G IN GAP

5   DURING FOUR years of warfare on the western front
the British cavalry had been seeking the gap and hoping to put
its gees through. The Germans had done it at the opening of the
war, but missed their chances and never seriously affected
the issue. After the transfer of the B.E.F. from the Aisne to
the north the British Cavalry Corps had a great measure of
success while the front remained fluid, but this had been
brought to an end as soon as the main bodies of the opposing
armies clashed at First Ypres. The French had been balked
time after time in Champagne. After that no real chance had
appeared until the end of 1917. How could this have been
possible when, for example, some days before the start of the
Battle of the Somme on July 1, 1916, a British artillery officer
in an observation post had counted, just south of the deep
Ancre Valley, sixteen aprons of wire covering the German
first line and an average of five rows along the second? The
former obstacle was in fact pretty well cut, but the latter
remained except here and there, and there were still more lines
out of range of the field artillery. At Arras Allenby's cavalry
had been foiled. At Cambrai there was a genuine chance, but
it was lost through the congestion of roads and tracks. In the
offensive known as the Battle of Amiens, beginning on August

3, 1918, the British cavalry did well enough, but cavalry and tanks cannot easily be co-ordinated, and the armor had over-whelmingly the major role.

The greatest services rendered by the cavalry had been, first, in holding the trenches in emergency; secondly, in its support of the tattered and broken infantry in the German offensive of March 1918, notably in a famous charge by troops of the 3rd Cavalry Division on March 24. Now, in Palestine, Yeomen, Indians, Australians—almost wholly "amateur" soldiers—and French colonials were to attempt to do that in which the British regular cavalry had so often been frustrated, to do what the Marquess of Granby had done at Warburg to have his name preserved on hundreds of inn signs all over England.

The head of the 4th Cavalry Division quitted its bivouac in the orange groves at 4 A.M., watered at the Wadi Auja—the troughs being later stacked in wagons—and moved at a walk to its position of assembly, and there unsaddled and fed the horses. Under the arrangement already described, Major-General Barrow rode into the captured position—it would have been unlike him to send a staff officer—and was told by Major-General Fane of the 7th Indian Division that he could now go through. He hurried back and ordered forward the 11th Cavalry Brigade, commanded by Brigadier-General C. L. Gregory.

The task of the 4th Cavalry Division was to penetrate by way of the Musmus Pass into the Plain of Esdraelon and cut the railway. The main body was with the least possible delay to swing right, make for the Jordan at Beisan, and send a detachment to secure the bridge, ten miles farther north, at Jisr el Majami.

The Turkish divisions in the plain had been routed and cleared off the path, so that there was no opposition at first and very little thereafter. "The great column streamed northward without even its vanguard being checked. For once, it seemed, the clock had been put back, and warfare had recovered in this splendid spectacle the pageantry whereof long-range weapons had robbed it. The hearts of all were high as they realized that the plan was unfolding perfectly. The two divisions were moving on parallel lines to the enemy's new flank and within a few hours would be behind him."[1]

The initial pace having been hot, an hour's rest was called at 1 P.M. On restarting, the division formed three brigade groups in echelon from the left: the 12th Brigade under Brigadier-General J. T. Wigan on the right, the 10th Brigade under Brigadier-General R. G. Howard-Vyse in the center, the 11th Brigade under Brigadier-General Gregory on the left. Shortly afterwards the 10th and 11th Brigades reached the Turkish third-line defenses, but did not encounter the first opposition. The Turkish depot regiment holding the position, which must have contained a high proportion of Arabs, had fled at top speed. A squadron of Jacob's Horse, which had started as advance guard to the division and was now leading the brigade, swept forward, secured 126 prisoners at once and brought the catch up to over 200 a little later. It was now nearing 4:30 P.M., and plentiful water having been found by two of the brigades, they made another halt. The 10th Brigade was less lucky, finding only two small wells. Howard-Vyse therefore decided to push on farther, leaving one regiment to water, so that his main body did not stop till 8:30 P.M. An hour or so later Major-General Barrow arrived and was told that, owing to the watering process being so slow, the brigade was unlikely to march again before 11:30. This would not do for the divisional commander, who felt that he must get the leading brigade through the pass as speedily as possible at all hazards. He bade the brigadier march by 11 P.M., water or no water. Meanwhile the brigade advanced guard, the 2nd Lancers, had ridden on into the pass.

The original intention had been that the lancers should await the remainder of the brigade within the entrance of the pass, but again this was not good enough for Barrow, who drove forward with a staff officer, Lieutenant-Colonel W. J. Foster. He was naturally worried about the prospect of his division's being held up by the enemy in the defiles beginning about halfway through.

The lancers had met no opposition and in fact had seen no Turks but for a couple of hundred transport men who surrendered at once, with a long column of wagons. The divisional commander arrived at 11:45 P.M. and ordered the regiment to push on to the *tell* below which lie the ruins of the city of Megiddo.* The regiment now put its light armored cars in the van and went on to reach its goal at 3:30 A.M. on September 20.

Barrow drove back to meet the main body of the brigade. Years after the war he was wont to declare that the ensuing quarter of an hour was the worst in his life. The 10th Brigade was not in sight, but had evidently lost its way and veered northward past the mouth of the pass. Barrow sent Foster off to find it and awaited his return, champing with impatience. At last the staff officer appeared on a horse—why he left the car behind is not known, but it had probably broken a spring on the bumpy ground. Foster had time to tell the divisional commander that the brigade was a good five miles away before he virtually collapsed with fatigue and vexation. Since Barrow had been accompanied only by his staff officer, he now mounted the horse and rode back alone.

First of all he met Wigan's 12th Brigade and directed him to replace the 10th and take the 2nd Lancers under his command. The delay had proved disturbing, just over two hours which might be vital. Wigan's leading regiment, the 6th Cavalry, did all it could to make up for the lost time, marching at the speed which best combined haste and the preservation of horseflesh: trotting twenty minutes, walking twenty, and halting five. It reached the exit from the Musmus Pass at 4:50 A.M.

Barrow now removed Howard-Vyse from his command and replaced him by Lieutenant-Colonel W. G. K. Green

---

* *Tell* means "mound," but virtually always one covering ruins. As all over the Middle East, one race or civilization has built on the ruins of the last, five layers being common.

of Jacob's Horse (11th Cavalry Brigade). Howard-Vyse was an officer of the Royal Horse Guards who had won a high reputation in this theater as the first chief of staff of the Desert Mounted Corps, in which, rightly or wrongly, it had been considered that Chauvel might need some coaching in the early days of his big command. (British commanders and staffs were inclined to be too patronizing in this respect, to the annoyance of Australians and Canadians.) Howard-Vyse was only thirty-five years of age and had shown himself equally at home on the staff and in this role when he had changed places with Brigadier-General C. A. C. Godwin. In character he was charming and had become a popular figure, known as "the Wombat" after the Australian marsupial, the nickname having apparently been taken from a polo pony.

Here was a case of shocking bad luck. The Musmus Pass is rather flattered by its title and its southern entrance is not altogether easy to hit, even in daylight, since here the flanking hills rise only a few feet above the grassy floor of the vale. Some men in his place would have felt bruised in spirit for life, but the Wombat never grumbled up to the day of his death, which occurred when this book was in the press.

The officer in command of the 2nd Lancers, Captain D. S. Davison, was the most fortunate of men. Both the commanding officer and second-in-command were sick, and the former's replacement did not arrive from England till September 23. Meanwhile Davison accomplished a feat such as a cavalryman might recall in his dreams for the rest of his life. He had already fed and watered the horses while his men breakfasted, so that, despite their arduous march, all were fit for new endeavors. Issuing from the pass at 5:30 A.M. on the 20th, the center squadron came upon a strong Turkish force which had not entered the pass but had deployed outside to prevent the British debouching into the plain. Davison ordered this squadron, with all the machine guns and the armored cars, to hold the enemy frontally, while the reserve squadron got on to his flank in a shallow but useful depression and charged him. While the squadron was on the move, the commander of the third

squadron, who was some distance from Captain Davison and
had received no order from him, saw what was going on and at
once decided to take part—an admirable piece of initiative
because the Turks were drawn up in two lines, which were
now to be attacked simultaneously.

One or two critics have underrated the brilliance of this
exploit on the ground that if the enemy had handled his
machine guns steadily in the tradition of Turkish troops the
charge would have failed with sickening loss. The answer
surely is, first, that the officers knew what had happened in
the infantry attack which had put the cavalry through and
that this had revealed widespread though not universal demoralization; secondly, that these well-trained troops and
horses could have swerved away if the fire had proved too hot
and accurate; thirdly, the weight of the covering fire from the
light armored cars and Hotchkiss machine guns was almost a
guarantee of success. How fit and gallant the horses were is
shown by the speed they could raise after covering over forty
miles in about twenty-five hours, but they were ridden by
excellent horsemen. The Indian cavalryman, spare of frame
and thin-legged, looked so well on a horse that many people
believed his seat to be natural, but in truth he had to be trained
carefully, after which he had the advantage of averaging some
fourteen pounds less than a British cavalryman.

The charge must have been a magnificent spectacle,
though it was witnessed only by the participants, only a handful of whom were British—and they have left no record but
a prosaic war diary—but those who have ridden a colt at a
jump neck-and-neck with a rival can readily imagine the wild
excitement of the sweating horses. The lance, when not in
action, was carried in a little stirrup-bucket, with a loop over
the rider's arm. In a charge it was held under the arm and
balanced by being gripped well forward of the butt. It was
deadly at close quarters, causing ugly wounds, frequently
mortal. The lance came in for mockery as the most obsolete of
weapons, but it was no more so than the sword and was a far
better weapon. Two of the Indian cavalry regiments which

were not lancers had begged that lances should be issued to them, had got them, and afterwards expressed greater confidence.

The fire of the Turkish machine guns was maintained almost until the moment of the shock, but the Turks were so shaken by the spectacle of their foes galloping in on either flank that most of the fire was high. Almost simultaneously, the two squadrons crashed home and rolled up both lines of the panic-stricken Turks. Forty-six were speared and virtually all the rest, numbering 470, taken prisoner. On their side the lancers had only a single man wounded and twelve horses killed.

This was a great feat of arms, and the fact that Davison had sent no order to the second squadron leader is immaterial; indeed he probably had no time to do so before the squadron moved. And, after all, Nelson at the Nile sent no order to his captains because they all knew his tactics thoroughly and went alongside the moored French ships according to his principles.

The unhappy Marshal Liman had, reasonably, hoped that the pass would be blocked. He got no word of what actually had happened until the afternoon, and then it must have come as a shock to him to discover that it was a German officer, Major Frey, who had let down his side by failing to reach a position within the pass. Indifferent as the troops were, if they had got in the pass they would surely have held up Davison until he was reinforced, which would have been a serious delay. The Turkish force was the 13th Depot Regiment at Nazareth, which Liman had ordered at 12:30 P.M. *on September 19* to occupy the pass, and it had to cover only fifteen miles. To Liman's natural astonishment, he met Frey as far away as Samakh and was told that the British had reached the exit before Frey could secure it.[2] How one would like to know what Liman said to him!

On went the lancers, to come under fire from El Affule. Their action here, however, proved to be secondary. The station had already been captured by a regiment of the 5th Cavalry Division, with 75 Germans and about 200 Turks as prisoners. Ten engines and four or five times as many trucks were taken, with three aircraft on the nearby airfield. Another airplane landed soon afterwards with a load of mail, useful material for the intelligence service when it had time to sort the correspondence. After the division had closed up, Barrow, at 1 P.M., ordered a march on Beisan, where it concentrated by 6 P.M. On the road the division captured several hundred more prisoners, and these represented the first handful seen of the fugitives from the infantry. It took another seven hundred-odd during the night.

The region was one that had been soaked in blood by many battles. Pharaoh Thothmes III had used the Musmus Pass and won at Megiddo a great victory over the King of Kadesh (today Homs). Saladin had overthrown the forces of the Latin Kingdom of Jerusalem at the Horns of Hattin, just off the road from Nazareth to Tiberias. The terrible Mongols had been routed and Egypt saved by the Mameluke Sultan Kutuz in the Valley of Jezreel. The young Bonaparte, hurrying from his lines in front of Acre, had rescued Kléber, when at his last gasp. More could be added, but the most famous scene is not that of a battle. It was here, on the slope of Mount Gilboa, that the watchman on the tower had cried out that the chariots speeding from the Jordan Valley must be those of Jehu the son of Nimshi.

Thomas Hardy wrote just afterwards:

Did they catch as it were in a Vision at shut of the day—
When their cavalry smote through the ancient Esdraelon Plain,
And they crossed where the Tishbite stood forth in his enemy's
way—
His gaunt mournful shade as he bade the King haste off amain?

On war-men of this end of time—even on Englishmen's eyes—
Who slay with their arms of new might in that long-ago place,
Flashed he who drove furiously? . . . Ah, did the fantom arise
Of that Queen, of that proud Tyrian woman who painted her
face?

Faintly marked they the words "Throw her down!" rise from
  Night eerily,
 Spectre spots of the blood of her body on some rotten wall?
And the thin note of pity that came: "A King's daughter is she,"
  As they passed where she trodden was once by the chargers'
   footfall?

Could such be the hauntings of men of today, at the cease
  of pursuit, at the dusk-hour, ere slumber their senses could seal?
Enghosted seers, kings, one on horseback who asked "Is it peace?"
  Yea, strange things and spectral may men have beheld in
   Jezreel![8]

The 4th Cavalry Division had marched 70 miles in 34 hours, foundering only twenty-six horses. This was a stupendous feat and an example of magnificent horsemastership. It will appear in the summing up of the Desert Mounted Corps' achievement that the division was well ahead of the other two in this respect, but it was not again called on to equal this. The Germans were proud that one of their divisions had, in the invasion of Belgium and France in 1914, covered 30 miles in a day, but it is not claimed they did it two days running, and the attached *Jäger* battalions would not in that case have been able to keep up. A good proportion of the march had been in the pleasant cool of the Palestinian early autumn night, but during the day the heat had been torrid. Little clouds from the sweating horses had hung over the columns, and the Yeomen, if not the Indians, had been considerably distressed, though there are no reports of their sleeping in the saddle and sometimes falling to the ground as had happened to mounted men in the retreat from Mons. They had outdistanced their transport by fifty miles—that night even the motor trucks got only as far as El Affule—but the men had their emergency ration and some fodder was found. All the horses were by this time near the end of their endurance. Fortunately all could now rest, with the exception of one regiment.

What the 19th Lancers of the 12th Cavalry Brigade lost in

horseflesh is unknown, but this regiment carried out an extra task which makes the record even more astonishing. Setting out at 7:30 P.M., the regiment reached Jisr el Majami at 5 A.M. on September 21 after a very arduous march of about twenty miles, six miles longer than that of the rest of the division. Whereas the division had followed a fairly good road, the lancers' all-night march was over very rough and stony ground. On arrival the regiment scattered the few enemy troops at the station. The party of Royal Engineers which accompanied the lancers placed explosive charges in the bridges over the Jordan and its tributary the Yarmuk, but did not blow them up in case they should be needed by British forces later on.

As has been pointed out, the 5th Cavalry Division had less reason to consult an infantry divisional commander before it took off than did the 4th, it being less likely to interfere with the infantry because the division was to begin its march along the beach, but that it had to make similar arrangements. Thus, at 7 A.M., Major-General Macandrew was informed by Major-General Shea, in command of the 60th Division, that shells had ceased to fall on the beach and that in his view the cavalry division could begin its advance. General Macandrew so informed the commander of his advanced guard, Brigadier-General P. J. V. Kelly, to whose 13th Cavalry Brigade the 7th Light Car Patrol and the 12th Light Armoured Motor Battery were attached.

Kelly was an outstanding figure and included fluent Arabic among his qualifications. As an officer of the 3rd Hussars, he had in 1916 defeated the sultan of the last independent Central African kingdom (except Abyssinia) and had been Sir Reginald Wingate's instrument in incorporating Darfur, west of Kordofan Province, into the Sudan. Ali Dinar had deserted the Khalifa on the night before Kitchener's victory in the Battle of Omdurman, or Khartoum, with several thousands of his slave army and had seized the capital of Darfur, the town of El Fasher, where Kitchener had given

him leave to proclaim himself sultan, paying a small annual
tribute, and where he had behaved himself reasonably well
until after the outbreak of the First World War. Then the influence of the Turks, exerted through the Senussi, had cor-
rupted him, and he had stopped paying the tribute. Even then
he was treated with forbearance until in late 1915 he was discovered to be planning an invasion of the Sudan to coincide
with an invasion of Egypt by the Senussi. Colonel Kelly had
sharply defeated him at Beringia, some 600 miles west of
Khartoum, and again at Jebel Juba, after he had fled from El
Fasher. Ali Dinar's retreat was turned into a panic by a few
small bombs dropped from a single aircraft by Lieutenant J. C.
Slessor, who was to end his career as marshal of the Royal Air
Force. Unable to keep the pursuit going, with little more than
150 rifles and one gun, Kelly had handed it over to Major
H. J. Huddleston, who has also made an appearance in this
narrative. A mile from Jebel Juba, Ali Dinar's body was found
shot through the head. Darfur was once more incorporated
into the Sudan.

The leading regiment, Hodson's Horse, went forward so
fast through the sand that Macandrew, galloping after the
regiment to check it, could not catch up. The horses were
being tried too heavily. How many horses the regiment had to
destroy is unknown, but certainly more than another regiment
of the brigade, the 18th Lancers, which shot five and left ten
more behind. It was a somewhat distressing start in the eyes of
a horsemaster such as Macandrew. However, adequate wells
were found and the brigade had a rest, not moving on again
until 6:15 P.M.

The brigade had now veered inland and was following
Napoleon's route to Acre, but presently quitted this to continue the march farther east. Kelly himself led the vanguard
and picked up an Arab who appeared to know something of
the country—though, as it proved, not much. The brigade was
now strung out, since it moved through the hills in single file,
and did not reach Abu Shushe till 2:15 A.M. on September 20,
where it halted to close up. Three quarters of an hour later the

brigade crossed the railway to Haifa and the engineers cut a breach in it. Another half hour, and the guide told the brigadier that the village ahead was Nazareth. This was a virtual impossibility. The brigade was still in the plains and Nazareth stands on the far side in the hills of Galilee, approached by hairpin bends. The brigade had, in fact, another four miles or more to go. However, Kelly thought it best to clear the village, in which operation he took 200 Turks in their sleep. He now ordered the Gloucester Hussars to act as advanced guard and make for Nazareth, as its horses were staunch enough to go forward at a trot. He had certainly made a mistake in dropping squadrons to clear this village and another further on, so that the brigade was very weak when it reached Nazareth at 4:30 A.M.

In those days Nazareth was notable as the best-built town in Palestine. Though well up in the hills, it lay in a cup-shaped depression. On the outskirts stood a large tourist hotel and, something over a quarter of a mile farther on, the Casa Nuova, a hospice where a religious order had in times of peace sheltered pilgrims. The hotel provided a staff mess and sleeping quarters, the Casa Nuova was the Turkish General Headquarters.

The leading troop galloped in without any special interest in these buildings, its sole objective being to capture the German commander-in-chief in his bed. And it very nearly succeeded. Liman's housekeeper related, in fact, that he had driven out in his pajamas. He says nothing of this himself, but he would not have been human if he had, and the good woman can hardly have invented the story. General Liman does say that he left the town and returned to direct the fighting.[4] This proved stiff indeed. The mess buildings were taken along with a big haul of prisoners. In other buildings used as offices many papers were seized, but the defenders managed to burn a great quantity, and the Casa Nuova could not be reached. The street fighting was ferocious, and if the staff officers were foremost in the fray, the German clerks also fought stoutly shoulder to shoulder with them until virtually annihilated.

The brigade had been instructed to fight its way either through or around the town in order to seal the roads to Tiberias and Acre, but it was so short of troops by reason of the dropped detachments that it found the task impossible. In any case the brigade had to devote a large proportion of troops to the town itself because Kelly had also been ordered to secure "important prisoners and important documents." Just before seven o'clock Kelly sent back a message to Macandrew that his hands were full of a horde of prisoners and begging Macandrew to push on the 14th Cavalry Brigade. The divisional commander sent back an orderly, who did not reach the scene until 10:55, with a note to the effect that the horses were too exhausted and that Kelly must withdraw to El Affule. The brigadier retreated in good order, having had unexpectedly light losses: those of the 18th Lancers are not known, but Hodson's Horse suffered only nine and the Gloucesters thirteen, the latter having twenty-eight horses killed.

Kelly now became the second cavalry brigadier to be removed from his command, and ill luck also played a part in his case. Such are the operational risks of warfare, and were so perhaps most of all in the days of horsed cavalry. Kelly was not dismissed on the spot as Howard-Vyse had been by his divisional commander—though this of course had to be approved by Allenby—but by the commander-in-chief himself after deliberation, because his case was more complex. Kelly had failed in judgment when he had stripped his brigade to clear the two villages held by a foe too shaken to fight.*

Unlike the 4th Cavalry Division, the 5th had operated on the front of a single brigade. There is thus no more to be said of it here, except that the divisional train did not arrive at El Affule until midday on September 21, having followed the 4th Cavalry Division through the Musmus Pass.

* Shortly before he began this chapter the writer received a letter from a British-born American citizen who served as a brigade signaler in the raid. He was an out-and-out admirer of the brigadier and asserted that Kelly had been handicapped, great delay having been caused by the inaction of a useless Egyptian signals company which did not pass a message through during two days.

The Australian Mounted Division, from which the 5th Light Horse Brigade was still detached, had several miles to cover from its assembly area before it reached the old front line. After a march of 28 miles the division bivouacked on the Nahr Iskanderune. Chauvel came up to it after his advanced headquarters, large in itself, had found difficulty in getting its cars over the rough and sandy ground. The total number of cars shifting corps headquarters with its numerous clerks, orderlies, and impedimenta was fifty.[5] Next day corps headquarters was established at Megiddo, in touch with GHQ and the three divisions by wireless and, if necessary, by aircraft. Chauvel ordered Major-General Hodgson to drop a regiment of the 4th Australian Light Horse Brigade as escort to the corps headquarters before moving through the Musmus Pass. Since the divisional commander had already detailed a second regiment to escort his transport and late in the night of September 19 was directed to send the rest of the brigade to seek out that of the 5th Cavalry Division and convoy it through the pass, Hodgson had now with him only the 3rd Light Horse Brigade and his divisional troops.

The reduced division moved off at 1 A.M. on September 20 and after one halt in the pass reached the Plain of Esdraelon, where Chauvel shortly came up with it again. At 2:45 P.M. an aircraft reported that the enemy was in flight from Jenin, whereupon Chauvel directed Hodgson to send a squadron to establish touch with the detached 5th Light Horse Brigade, which he believed to be moving on Jenin from the south. It will, however, be recalled that the 5th Brigade's commander, Brigadier-General Onslow, had decided that the delays to which he had been subjected had made it impossible to take the place while daylight lasted and he had returned to Tul Karm. Hodgson ordered the 3rd Light Horse Brigade to march due southeast on Jenin. Brigadier-General L. E. Wilson, the brigade commander, was as reliable a man as could have been allotted the task, but a strange contrast to his flamboyant troops, all-state countrymen. He was a small, shy, and modest

Brisbane solicitor, but not without experience of war, since he had served as a trooper in South Africa.[6]

The brigade advanced at a trot, but soon afterwards the 10th Australian Light Horse Regiment, anxious not to incur the fate of the 5th Brigade and be caught by the fall of darkness, speeded up to a gallop and covered 11 miles in 70 minutes— not bad for horses in the condition earlier described of those in the division. About three miles from Jenin the vanguard saw a large body of Turks in a grove, whereupon a single squadron peeled off, deployed, and galloped at them. The Turks had been awaiting attack from the south and were completely surprised. Nearly 1,860 men, a fair number of them Germans, surrendered. Odds of at least fifty to one! At Jenin there was resistance, but only from a party of Germans, who first opened machine-gun fire from the windows and then strove to fight their way out but were overwhelmed.

Great quantities of stores were found by the troops when they could attend to them, encumbered as they were with about 3,000 prisoners, but by that time much had been looted by the townsmen. One item was 120 cases of German champagne—which existed long before the days of Ribbentrop— over which a guard was placed and a fair proportion issued to the troops, though there is reason to suppose the Australians missed no opportunities before the guard was mounted. Another item was a bullion wagon, the contents of which were to prove useful in buying food and fodder.

"Pandemonium broke out in the town. Screaming 'Arab! Arab!' as if this were a password with the Australians to allow them to loot, men, women and children threw themselves on the immense stores of food, clothing, and equipment stacked in sheds or piled on the transport which was blocked in the narrow street. Dumps at the station and elsewhere were set alight before the arrival of the brigade and were burning too fiercely to be saved. As darkness fell, the place was lit up by their glare, and the moon arose upon a scene of frenzy like one of the sacks of German towns in the Thirty Years' War—

save that here the peaceful inhabitants played the part of despoilers instead of that of victims."[7]

The 10th Light Horse Regiment now moved south to a point where the issues from the Judaean hills dropped towards the plain, supported by a machine-gun subsection under the command of Lieutenant R. R. W. Patterson. The latter, however, lost his way and reached the road ahead of the regiment. Immediately afterwards he came on a long column, its strength being apparent rather to the ear, by the tramp of feet on the metalled road, than to the eye. Patterson opened fire on the column, and when the troops at the head of the column began to deploy, he rode forward and shouted to them to surrender. With the head of the column was a German nurse who spoke good English, and she translated to the officers Patterson's bluff that he was supported by a large force. So 2,800 men surrendered to 23 Australians.[8]

The total prisoner haul was now about 25,000; the Turkish Eighth Army, with the exception of Colonel von Oppen's corps, had been almost destroyed; the Seventh Army was little better off, even though the majority were still free men. It must have been just before this time that Chauvel told Allenby he had 13,000 prisoners. The commander-in-chief answered with a laugh: "No bloody good to me! I want 30,000 from you before you've done."[9] He was to get many more.

On quitting Nazareth finally Liman drove to Tiberias, where he arrived at 3:30 P.M. He had no staff but General Kiazim and two orderly officers who had accompanied him. After giving what instructions seemed feasible for the defense of the town he went on to Samakh. His one object now was to hold the line of the Jordan between Lake Hula and the Sea of Galilee and above all Jisr Benat Yakub ("Bridge of the Daughters of Jacob") while the retreating troops fell back on the gorge of the Yarmuk and the railway from Samakh to Dera, where he moved after midnight. His one crumb of comfort was that Oppen's rear guard was fighting on. It was useless for the commander-in-chief to remain on what was already a battlefield, since the Arabs attacked it on September 20, so next day he established his headquarters at Damascus. He was enlivened by a "fantasia" by Druses from the Hauran, who would have aided him had he been able to support them. He also received a telegram asking him to give a prize for a sack race in Constantinople, but did not comply, feeling that he himself was engaged in one.[10]

Liman still hoped to save something out of the wreck. He even envisaged a counterattack—one might almost call it a counteroffensive—and a breakout northward on a large scale. He knew that both Beisan and El Affule were strongly held, but there appeared to be only one Light Horse brigade in the fifteen miles between them. He issued orders to Colonel von Oppen to strike with all his own troop strength and any other troops he could rally; the commander of the Asia Corps accepted the task with no apparent hesitation, and all seemed well. Then, however, there occurred what a close observer calls the "highly dramatic night" of September. He describes it thus not so much because the orders were canceled as for Oppen's indecision, "a strange contrast to his wonted calm and deliberation." What had happened was that Oppen's staff officers had persuaded him that the risks were too great. Liman was annoyed, considering that he was wrong and that he would have saved many more men if he had stuck to the plan instead of heading for the Jordan. Simon-Eberhard could not decide whether the commander-in-chief or the Eighth Army commander, who had backed Oppen, was right.[11]

Nazareth, now emptied of its defenders, was occupied on September 21. From Jenin 7,000 more captives marched out. The Germans marched proudly at the head of the column and showed their discipline by goose-stepping whenever a car carrying a general's pennon passed by. Another 8,000 were brought back next day through the Musmus Pass.

It was a matter of urgency to secure Haifa and Acre as soon as possible in order to land supplies from the sea, but an abortive peck with light armored and unarmored cars led to a delay of twenty-four hours. Greater strength was obviously needed, and on September 23 the task was allotted to the 5th Cavalry Division. The division moved in two columns, the 13th Cavalry Brigade on the right against Acre, the 15th Cavalry Brigade, commanded by Brigadier-General C. R. Harbord, on the left against Haifa, followed by the rest of the division. Acre was taken almost without opposition, but Haifa looked to be a far more serious matter. The main road from El Affule ran for miles along the foot of Mount Carmel and was commanded by it, but there was also a pack track along the crest—which was known to be flat and which was to be used by a single squadron of the Mysore Lancers—to supply food to a big religious pension, the *Karmelheim.*

The regiment, less this detachment, came under machine-gun fire both along the main road and from the artillery near this building. A second lancer squadron later climbed the steep rise to aid the squadron already on top, followed by one of the Sherwood Rangers from the 14th Brigade, and a battery of the Honourable Artillery Company went into action. The charge of the leading Mysore squadron was a truly astonishing spectacle. Owing to a number of horses having dropped out lamed or having been hit, there were only about fifteen mounted men left. Yet, charging home, they routed the defense. One point not often recognized is that even mortally wounded horses may reach their objective in a short charge. The town was taken equally quickly. Captures amounted to 689 and sixteen guns. The casualties were 37 (only three killed), but the loss in horses, 60 killed and 83 wounded, was heavy. However, some good remounts were taken to replace them. This scintillating little victory was won by boldness, speed, and quick thinking.

Let it be owned that Allenby had made one mistake: he had blocked the roads to the north this side of Jordan and the Wadi Fara, but he had left a gap of some twenty miles between it and the positions held south of Beisan, and through it the Turks and Oppen's Germans were streaming. They would still have a practicable road to Damascus running west of Dera. Chauvel's quick action repaired almost all the damage. He ordered the 4th Cavalry Division to block the escape by moving on both sides of the river, and Barrow entrusted the task to his 11th Cavalry Brigade.

Two squadrons of Jacob's Horse charged a Turkish force approaching a ford and overwhelmed it, taking 800 prisoners, including a Turkish divisional commander. Then the Turks proved that they were by no means all demoralized. Two batteries for a time shot with great gallantry and hit three British guns, which were forced to withdraw, though not put out of action.[12] The Turks did not, however, withstand a mounted charge, followed by all-round pressure which netted a haul bringing the day's prisoners to some 4,000. It was now evening, and since the horses had last watered at Beisan, they were utterly exhausted and needed a night's rest.

On the morning of September 24 Lieutenant-Colonel E. F. Lawson, commanding the Middlesex Yeomanry, ordered a squadron to forestall the enemy at another ford. Lawson's original regiment was the Bucks Yeomanry, which had now gone to France. He can hardly be called an amateur soldier, because his greatest prewar and even postwar interest was in his regiment, which between the wars was converted to artillery. Lawson was a man of outstanding ability and courage and was to distinguish himself in command of divisional artillery in the retreat to Dunkirk in 1940, after rising to the highest administrative post on what had formerly been a family newspaper, *The Daily Telegraph*. His death followed that of Howard-Vyse while this book was in the press. Though the squadron failed to beat the Turks to the ford, it was speedily taken with the aid of reinforcements sent by Brigadier-General Gregory. On the east bank Jacob's Horse sealed the victory, and in all 5,000 prisoners were taken. A Turkish divisional commander was so distressed by the spectacle that he turned his back and exclaimed: "I cannot watch

any longer."[13] Nothing remained except a handful in hiding
and a body of the Asia Corps which had for the most part
crossed before the brigade arrived.[14]

Meanwhile the Australian Mounted Division had been
ordered to take Samakh and thus break Liman's rearguard
position. The 4th Light Horse Brigade, commanded by
Brigadier-General W. Grant, who had led the charge at
Beersheba, had to do the job with little more than half its
strength. Grant started at 2:30 A.M. on September 25, but
darkness served him well because the ground was flat as a
pancake. By 4:30 A.M. the 11th Light Horse Regiment came
under heavy machine-gun fire. One of the squadron leaders
shouted: "What orders, Colonel?" and was answered: "Form
line and charge the guns!" One squadron swung left-handed
into the village, another went around the station. Germans
and Turks fought hard, but the Australians would not be
denied. Things went better for them when machine-gun fire
drove the Germans from the windows, but the struggle was
fierce until the whole hostile force had been killed or taken.
The brigade had 14 killed and 29 wounded; 61 horses killed
and 27 wounded, about half the animals. Ninety-eight corpses
were found, and 23 officers and 341 rank and file were taken,
about 150 of these being German. Grant's achievement equaled
his dash at Beersheba and the heroic leadership of the defense
by *Hauptmann* von Keyserling lived up to the finest traditions of the German army.[15] Finally, a squadron skirted the
lake toward Tiberias and took it before the troops of Wilson's 3rd Light Horse Brigade arrived from the west in the
early hours of September 26. This time the almost unresisting
garrison was mostly Turkish, only 26 Germans surrendering
as against 75 Turks. One sad incident marred the occasion. A
white flag was displayed and, as invariably happens, was taken
as a signal of surrender. It seems impossible to make other
ranks or even the majority of junior officers understand that
a white flag betokens a request for a parley. Because fire was
resumed a number of men were killed in cold blood.[16]

One of Wilson's troops rode over the very ground of Saladin's victory, the Horns of Hattin.[17] In this small country of innumerable wars history has no difficulty in repeating itself.

CHAYTOR ACHIEVES MUCH WITH LITTLE

6 THE COMMANDER in the Jordan Valley was a cool man, short and sturdy in build, efficient and energetic. A lover of England and comfortably well off, Major-General Sir E. W. C. Chaytor was to acquire after the war an estate in the Old Country. Here, in the Jordan Valley, he was to prove his mettle.

General Chaytor received few orders from Allenby because his action depended on that of the Turks. Until their Fourth Army moved up along the Hejaz Railway, which it was certain to do when the advance of the Desert Mounted Corps threatened its communications, there was virtually nothing he could do. Jemal Pasha in fact waited two days too long in loyalty to his troops south of Amman.

On September 17 and 18 the British mounted troops probed the enemy's position. Next day the 2nd British West Indies Regiment of Brigadier-General E. R. B. Murray's 20th Indian Brigade was ordered to attack the enemy's positions in the hills of Transjordan. The regiment made a dashing advance under heavy fire and captured a formidable ridge. On September 20 the 1st Battalion did equally well; but the Jewish battalion, known as the 38th Royal Fusiliers, could not face the Turkish machine guns.

Chaytor now felt certain that the Turks were about to begin their withdrawal and that the time was come to secure the crossing at Jisr ed Damiye. On September 21 the Auckland Regiment found the enemy covering this, but was not strong enough to push him back. Chaytor therefore directed the remainder of the brigade, under Brigadier-General W. Meldrum, to attack, reinforced with two West Indian battalions. The column moved out along with the Inverness Battery of the Royal Horse Artillery and the 29th Indian Mountain Battery at 9 P.M.

On the next day General Meldrum's force surprised a Turkish column crossing the Jordan, but the Aucklands were counterattacked with great dash and driven back. Meldrum, needing infantry firepower, hurried on the 1st British West Indies Regiment, but before it reached the scene the Wellington Regiment had made some progress and captured several hundred prisoners. However, another Turkish column now appeared from the Wadi Fara and yet another began to cut behind the brigade. It looked as though Meldrum's force was about to be squeezed between the two Turkish columns and the prospect was not a pretty one, since the Turks numbered well over two thousand. Chaytor ordered up the 1st Australian Light Horse Brigade, and its mere presence sufficed to dispose of the threat. Meldrum thereupon launched a bayonet attack with a very small force—the Aucklands, a squadron of the Canterbury Regiment, and a company of the 1st British West Indies—which sheared through the Turkish rear guard. The enemy lost 786 prisoners, including the commander of the 53rd Division, and six guns, though a far larger body managed to cross.

Now was the time to penetrate into the hills through Es Salt—by a road which covered about twice as many road miles as air miles—to Amman, while a smaller force could move by tracks farther south as a right flank guard. Before the advance could begin, however, Chaytor had to withdraw a company and some machine guns from each of his eight infantry battalions. The 20th Brigade was to follow the Es Salt road and to have the support, if required, of the heavy artillery, amounting to one British battery and a section of captured 150 mm. howitzers, while the New Zealand Brigade was to make its way by the track from Jisr ed Damiye and take Es Salt if possible before the infantry arrived. The Jewish battalions, grouped under the senior commanding officer, Lieutenant-Colonel J. H. Patterson, as "Patterson's Column," were eventually to follow the 20th Brigade. Patterson became well known as a brilliant writer, and among his books is an enthusiastic account of the prowess of these troops, to which other observers make certain reservations.

As the sun rose on September 23 it could be seen that the enemy had everywhere abandoned the Jordan Valley and by dusk it was certain that he did not mean to fight on the escarpment. By 6:30 P.M. the 20th Brigade was well into the foothills. Only the New Zealanders met with some resistance, but this did not even slow their advance and they entered Es Salt at 4:20 P.M. In the town and at a redoubt just outside between 650 and 750 prisoners were taken, but these were almost all transport men, clerks, and orderlies, or stragglers and deserters. Welcome supplies were found here. Patterson's Column, exhausted by clearing the Jordan banks, arrived in the small hours of September 24.

Chaytor was awakened to receive orders from GHQ to do his utmost to prevent the Turks from quitting Amman for the north, but for once they had carried out excellent demolition work on the Jisr ed Damiye–Es Salt–Amman roads. A party one hundred strong of the Auckland Regiment, to which all the best horses in the regiment had been issued, was sent forward to cut the railway five miles north of Amman and returned within eleven hours after covering twenty miles.[1]

Australian and New Zealand regiments had come to the Middle East as good horsemen, but not, the former in particular, good horsemasters, because the men from upcountry had been used to riding three or four horses a day, turning each into a corral without a glance. Here, they had soon become expert in caring for their horses. The Desert Mounted

Corps did not believe in having horses bigger than the "riders" for the artillery, but frequently changed them round. Many horses must have been saved by this policy.

At 6 A.M. on September 25 the division began its advance on Amman: 2nd Light Horse Brigade on the right, New Zealand Brigade on the left, 1st Light Horse Brigade combining the functions of reserve and left flank guard. Turkish posts outside the town were easily scattered, but the opposition became stern at the approaches. General Borton, however, had warned Chaytor that one of his aircraft had reported the Turkish Fourth Army to be leaving Amman and that every effort would be made by bombing to slow its withdrawal. This was naturally not quite as effective as in the Judaean hills; but while the enemy had no defiles to pass through, he had no cover either. Bombs were also dropped on Amman itself.[2] The Turkish rear guard was fighting stoutly—and, as it proved, sacrificially—to save the main body, and the attacking force disposed of two mountain batteries only.

On getting to close quarters the Canterbury Regiment tried a mounted assault, but was held by the machine guns in the Citadel, which had saved Amman in the recent raid. The regiment then dismounted and this time took the place with the bayonet. Simultaneously the 2nd Light Horse Brigade, under Brigadier-General G. de L. Ryrie, closed up and overran the Turkish *sangars*—stone breastworks familiar in Indian frontier warfare—timing and driving home his attack in the style to which his own men in particular and all the troops of the division in general had long grown accustomed.

Though he had the least complex of characters, there is more to be said of General Ryrie than of any other Australian in this theater. In the first place, he was the most typical and representative bushman. As horseman and horsemaster he stood alone because he could throw and treat a sick horse as expertly as a veterinary officer. He was now fifty-five years old, an age at which in this stage of the war most men were cast like old horses; but no one dreamt of superannuating him.

He weighed over 200 pounds but rode astonishingly light, and even when he was not astride his best charger, a thorough-bred named Plain Bill, he did not distress his mounts as much as many men of 170 pounds. At home he was the equal of the aborigine with the boomerang, and he was a first-class heavy-weight boxer who still retained an astonishing speed and had lost none of his punch. His eye for country was superb. In his days as a politician he had proved to be an excellent actor in a rough and ready way. When he was first a candidate for the Australian Parliament his success had been largely due to his ability to entertain with appropriate music.

"When Ryrie first stood for Parliament he went round the electorate entertaining his audiences with a programme of rollicking ballads sung to his own accompaniment on a piano, a concertina, or any other musical instrument available. He was then, as he is now in 1922, capable of effective, bluff speech, marked by refreshing humour, courage, and common sense."[3]

Curiously enough, when he was on leave in England during the Battle of Rumani his place had been taken by the South African Brigadier-General J. R. Royston, who was the nearest to him in build and character, an even older man, and actually, though a "foreigner," even more popular with the Light Horse; but Royston had, as far over military age, been allowed to return to business affairs in the autumn of 1917. Ryrie had distinguished himself at First Gaza and had been disgusted by the premature order to withdraw. He was no student of the principles of war and he had paid scant attention even to handbooks on tactics, but his instinct was unsurpassed and it was said of him that he had never made a serious error in a campaign in which the mounted troops had to take exceptionally heavy risks. His was a fascinating mentality, with an amazing fund of spiritual and physical power.

On the capture of the *sangars*, though they were of no importance by comparison with the Citadel, the defense cracked and at 1:30 P.M. the 5th Light Horse entered Amman almost simultaneously with the Canterbury Regiment, heading for the railway station, which lay a mile or so east of what was then a small and sordid town. The last defenders were chased out, and the civil authorities approached Ryrie with a white flag. The captures amounted to 2,563 prisoners, ten guns, and about 300 horses. There was no sign of shortages in Amman, where plenty of forage was found in the barns, and cattle and sheep could be bought if the purchaser chose to pay enough. It should be noted that—though looting, hardly ever on a big scale, was not unknown, and never has been in any war—the army regularly paid its way. The chief motive was practical: the fellahin did not hide their grain and meat when they found it was paid for, and were readier to take up arms if called on when British friendship proved to be material as well as sentimental.

A fair proportion of the garrison had got away by train, though there were a number of breaches to the north which would compel detrainment. They were to be dealt with by the main body of the army and the Arabs, while Chaytor blocked the troops from Ma'an, 140 miles to the south. His troops were fast coming down with malaria in a region where it was endemic and no precautions against it were taken, but their strength lasted long enough to close the campaign triumphantly. Patrolling the railway northward, they found on September 28, at a station thirty miles from Amman, a Red Crescent train full of wounded and several ammunition trains. The Ma'an garrison was sighted from the air on the same day, and a message was dropped that it would be bombed on the morrow if it did not surrender. The Turks were also told that all water supplies within their reach were covered.

The first contact was made on September 29 when the 5th Light Horse reached a position less than half a mile from the Turkish advanced guard. Shortly afterwards a trolley ran up the line and an officer brought Lieutenant-Colonel D. C. Cameron a letter from the Turkish corps commander requesting that a meeting should be arranged. Before this could be done, however, there came from the Turk another letter stating that he wanted to surrender, but feared that his troops would be slaughtered by the Arabs if he did, since a single Australian regiment could obviously afford no protection. "On the hills east and west of the railway station hundreds of men mounted on horses and camels could be seen: their patient, watchful attitude suggesting the spectacle of vultures attending on a dying man."[4]

Cameron at once sent an officer forward, who returned with a message from Colonel Ali Bey, the Turkish commanding officer, that he surrendered unconditionally and would hand over guns, ammunition and stores to the victors, with the proviso that they should not enter his lines until they had mustered strength sufficient to protect him and his soldiers, particularly the sick and wounded. The Bedouin did not venture to envelop their expected prey on the northern side where the small body of Australians stood, but from the east, south, and west they were already attacking. The Turks held them off without much difficulty, but a tragedy seemed inevitable when, at 2:45 P.M., Cameron learned that the planned bombing attack had not been canceled for certain because the message might not have reached the RAF. He did some quick thinking, and directed that the groundsheet marking the report center on which messages were dropped should be taken into the Turkish defense position. Ali Bey expressed his gratitude and added that if the air attack were not stopped it would be the will of God. Turkish phlegm at its best!

The telephone line, which followed the railway, had been cut at three or four points but had been mended by the signalers, so that Chaytor learned what was afoot and communication with the Turks could be hastened. By 3:30 P.M. Cameron heard that the air attack was off. He ordered the Turks to hold their trenches all night in case the reinforcements had not arrived by last light. By this time the Ma'an garrison was nearly prostrated with fatigue and anxiety. It certainly could not have marched back to Ma'an without a rest even if the way had been free and the town unoccupied, but every man knew that it had been entered by the Arab regulars, and the men dreaded that they would be handed over to these birds of prey. Shrieks resounded in the desert air as groups of stragglers were caught and slaughtered, or carried off. Cameron naturally was well received by the Arabs, but they insisted that they had the right of allies to seize the arms of the common enemy. Losing his temper, Cameron warned them that if the attacks continued he would open fire. Things went more quietly thereafter, but he had to ward off a few dangerous isolated Arab thrusts.

Just as the Turkish chief of staff came out under a flag of truce Chaytor arrived on the scene and told the Turk that the reinforcements could not arrive before dark and that he might therefore hold his trenches till morning and not lay down his arms until then, but on no account were these to be rendered useless. Ali Bey was to come to Chaytor as a hostage, a practice which the Turks understood. Ali Bey was, however, not easily brought to leave his troops after his aide-de-camp had driven Cameron to fetch him because he considered his presence an additional guarantee of their safety, and he was not finally persuaded until the divisional commander himself arrived. Ali Bey told Chaytor that he would much prefer that the Australians should stand off and let him smash up the enemy. "That suggestion might in other circumstances have appealed to Chaytor, who was strong in his respect for the Turk and his scorn for the Arab, but it was impossible at the time, and the New Zealand leader, for once baffled, withdrew and left the situation to Ryrie."[5]

Chaytor could not have delegated it to a better man, and Ryrie's audacious solution of the problem may have saved thousands of lives. When he got the message he had only the 7th Australian Light Horse Regiment at hand. Alternately cantering and trotting; then galloping when Cameron sent word that matters were critical, he covered fifteen miles. Once again the Arab sheiks urged that the Australians should join them in an assault, and once again their plea was refused. Ryrie came to the decision that he must ally himself with Ali Bey for one night. Ordering two of the sheiks to ride with him, he galloped at the head of his two regiments through the Arab *enceinte* into the Turkish lines. On dismounting, his first action was to tell his two hostages that, if their followers attacked, they would instantly be shot. That this threat was bluff is sufficiently proved by the fact that it was never carried out, even though some of the Arabs did from time to time show signs of fresh aggression. No serious attack was, however, launched. Ryrie's conduct was extraordinarily bold, since it might just possibly have resulted in a partial and temporary breakout by the Turks and have involved some further loss to the Australians, in which case he would probably have been relieved of his command.

So Australians and Turks shared one another's campfires and food, heating chappaties together, and each reposing complete confidence in the honor of his enemy. The Australians enjoyed themselves immensely, feeling that they could leave the defense to the Turks, though they would have intervened quickly enough had it been necessary. They sang songs and, watching the anxieties of their temporary allies, shouted encouragement as the latter worked their machine guns and fired bursts of musketry. "Go on, Jacko!" they roared. "Give it to the blighters!"[6] So the discreet historian, but "blighters" was certainly not the term employed. In the morning the New Zealand Brigade reached the scene and the Turks began their march to Amman.

First of all, however, Ryrie took an even bolder step. Having concentrated the prisoners at the station, he took their rifle bolts, but directed two crack regiments of Anatolians to keep theirs, along with full bandoliers, in case of an attack on the march. He left the New Zealand Brigade to guard the sick, the wounded, and the booty until the rail line was repaired and the Turkish trains could take them on, but he mounted the worst cases on the camel *cacolets* of a Light Horse field ambulance.[7]

The 5th Australian Light Horse Regiment marched off to Amman with 4,068 prisoners, leaving 534 sick to be brought on by the railway trains. At this point 14 guns, 3 engines, and

25 railway trucks had also been taken, though the Turks had demolished a large number. From first to last Chaytor's force had taken 10,322 prisoners, 57 guns, 11 engines, and 106 railway carriages and trucks, plus many motor vehicles. Thousands of Arab soldiers in the Turkish service had slipped away to their homes. Next day their representatives came to Chaytor to find out his views about these men. He replied, to their joy, that so long as they kept quiet they would not be molested.

The sight of the two fine Turkish units marching proudly into Amman, fully armed, created a brief sensation. This must have been one of the most satisfactory incidents in Ryrie's career, and seldom can a brigadier have taken upon himself such heavy responsibilities. For Chaytor, too, the operation had been a triumph. His losses had been 3 officers and 24 other ranks killed, 10 officers and 95 other ranks wounded, and 7 men missing. The lion's share of the merit must go to him, but the staffwork was even above the average, the greatest weight having fallen on the shoulders of his chief staff officer, Lieutenant-Colonel J. A. Browne. The determination of the troops did the rest, and here a special tribute is owed to the 2nd British West Indies Regiment, which suffered well nigh a third of the losses in the whole force.

In November Chaytor temporarily withdrew his troops to Jerusalem and Bethlehem, where the diseases, above all malaria, inherited from the Turks swept through the ranks. The Australians and New Zealanders suffered worse than the men of the West Indies and the Jews. The most unfortunate would appear to have been the 1st and 2nd Light Horse Brigades, the only troops in the theater engaged from the day when Murray's forces first advanced across the Suez Canal.

UNLEASHING OF THE ARABS

7 THE PART PLAYED BY the Arab forces under the control of the Emir Feisal and Lawrence has not been touched on, except for the role of the Bedouin at Amman, and these were under nobody's control. First of all the relationship between Lawrence and the commander-in-chief should be made clear, and this is possible despite Allenby's uncommunicative nature. Allenby had, so to speak, inherited Lawrence from his predecessor and knew that Murray had thought a lot of him, but it was Allenby's wont to test opinions of this sort. In this case he did it largely by personal contact. To say that they became personal friends would be an exaggeration, though Lawrence did become his warm admirer, and Allenby, in his turn, came to the conclusion that, if he undertook a task, no one was more likely to carry it out successfully than Lawrence. There is no doubt that Lawrence could speak to Allenby with a confidence and hardihood not permitted in any other officer of his rank, but they were not on any such terms of familiarity as has sometimes been asserted. Allenby considered that the capture of Dera at the earliest possible date was vital to the success of his offensive and that Lawrence was by far the most likely—perhaps the only—agent to achieve it.

It had not taken Allenby long to reach this view. Even

before the capture of Jerusalem in December 1917 he had talked to Lawrence of the seizure of Dera and ordered him reconnoiter it, leaving to him the decision whether or not he should enter the town. At that time Allenby could not, of course, take into account the possibility that the continuance of his offensive would be balked by the exceptionally bad weather which followed or that he would have to strip his forces to reinforce the western front in the face of the German offensive of the following March.

It was a perilous assignment. Lawrence's Arabic, though fluent and scholarly, was not that of a native and could generally be detected as that of a stranger. Even if the garrison was wholly Turkish, with only a smattering of Arabic, there would be Arabs attached as servants, translators, and perhaps interpreters. But first-line soldiers live in peril, and it was vital to obtain the fullest possible information about the strength, armament, and dispositions of the garrison. The story of what followed is prickly in the extreme, but, apart from Lawrence's own account in *The Seven Pillars of Wisdom*, it has already been told by the Frenchman Beraud-Villars, Anthony Nutting, and others. Terence Rattigan has actually staged it in his brilliant *Ross* with remarkable candor and it has been filmed in *Lawrence of Arabia* with what many think to be horrific detail.

The occasion on which Allenby gave his instructions was one in which he was at his most critical and sceptical, that in which he asked Lawrence "what his railway efforts meant, or rather if they meant anything beyond the melodramatic advertisement they gave to Feisal's cause."[1] Lawrence set out with Talal, the sheik of Tafas, a village a few miles north of Dera, who was said to have killed twenty-three Turks with his own hand. After some days of scouting, Lawrence decided to enter Dera in rags and alone, since Talal was too well known.[2]

On the outskirts of the town Lawrence was challenged and arrested by a sergeant, who did not think he was a spy but took him for a deserter. Lawrence, with his usual presence of mind, declared he was a Circassian, an excellent plea, since the Circassians were small fair-haired men like himself and not called on for active military service because they already fulfilled the functions of a resident Turkish garrison. These people had been brought, generally in families, from Russia, and later reinforced by parties riding through on their own initiative. Settled in small communities dotted over the country, especially east of the Jordan, they had effectively kept down their Arabic neighbors. They were good fighters and most intelligent, as is proved again today by the fact that some of the best officers in the forces of King Hussein of Jordan are Circassians.

Unhappily for Lawrence, however, the Turkish sergeant was uninterested in his prisoner's nationality, did not bother to question him, and took him straight into Dera to the headquarters and into the Governor's bedroom. Nahi Bey was in his nightgown. He laid hold of Lawrence, and, when Lawrence broke loose, summoned the guard to strip him. Lawrence's last resort after being pawed revoltingly was to knee the Governor in the groin, and while he squirmed in agony the soldiers flogged their prisoner until he fainted. On coming to, Lawrence was locked in another room, from which he escaped at dawn.

As stated, this incident is described by several writers, but no two of them agree on its significance or indeed on the truth of his own account. It has been taken as proof that Lawrence was a homosexual. He was himself partially to blame by reason of some remarks he made about his sensations at the time. The balance of opinion and probability is that he did not come even into the milder category of homosexuality. There would be no reason to discuss the matter in a historical study, however important it might be in a biography, were it not for the fact that it influenced him and affected his future so strongly. He was lacerated in mind as well as body. His hatred of the Turks became frenzied. It was to be exhibited on the very ground where he had suffered this indignity. It has been asserted that he still felt his wounds when he took part in Allenby's entry into Jerusalem. He had by then been promoted to the rank of major on the staff, and, he tells us, "Dalmeny lent me red tabs, Evans his brass hat."[3]* It was just after this event that Lawrence first met Chaim Weizmann, the father of Zionism, and felt an immediate liking for him. Lawrence was not anti-Jewish, as Wingate proclaimed, whereas Wingate was bitterly anti-Arab, but Lawrence lived long enough to realize that the Jews were threatening the future of the Arabs in Palestine.

Lawrence's temper was not improved by the failure of the Arabs to co-operate in the second raid over the Jordan in late April and early May. A powerful tribe whose main camping ground lay in the hills volunteered to co-operate with the British, and Allenby not only accepted the offer but cherished the hope that it would be of considerable value. When the time came they failed to move. Lawrence considered that he had not been consulted soon enough and that the business had in consequence been muddled. However, Allenby did not lose confidence in him, which was what mattered.

Lawrence and the Arabs were taking on a heavy task, since they had not merely to tackle Dera but to deal with it between two and four days before the offensive started. This was essentially a task for trained troops, and if proof were needed that Lawrence had some able colleagues acting in liaison with the Arabs, it is to be found in the efficiency with

* Brigadier-General E. Evans was Deputy Adjutant and Quartermaster-General (chief administrative staff officer) of the XXI Corps. Dalmeny is the present Lord Rosebery. His younger brother, Neil Primrose, who had quitted his appointment as Under-Secretary of State for Foreign Affairs to fight, had been killed in the famous charge at Maghar in November 1917 in the course of the advance up the coast plain. His cousin, Major Evelyn de Rothschild, second-in-command of the same regiment, the Bucks Yeomanry, died of his wounds, so that two members of the great Jewish family were the only officers killed in this cavalry action just as the force entered the area of the Jewish colonies which it had founded. The regiment was led by Lieutenant-Colonel F. H. Cripps, elder brother of Stafford Cripps, the future Labor Chancellor of the Exchequer. Since Lieutenant-Colonel E. F. Lawson, whose exploits at the Jordan fords have been recorded, was then a captain in the Bucks, the regiment had an exceptional number of distinguished officers.

which this task of organizing "regular" contingents from people unaccustomed to this type of warfare was accomplished.
This was a task for which Lawrence, an "irregular" in every
fibre, was unfitted. When the troops had been formed, however, he knew how to employ them. First, of course, they
needed a base of operations. Right out in the desert sixty miles
to the southeast, he found an ideal one, where a landing ground
for aircraft could easily be prepared. Qasr el Azraq was a
Roman fort standing amidst big pools of pure water and shaded
by palms. The building provided shelter for provisions which
could easily be guarded from the irregular soldiery who were
to follow. These irregulars were to include some of the best
leaders and fighting men of their kind. Auda Abu Tayi brought
his Howeitat tribesmen; Talal his fellahin of the Hauraun;
Nuri esh Shalaan, a formidable veteran and one of the greatest
of the desert sheiks, his Rualla. Auda had begun by siding with
the Turks, or at least going through the motions of so doing,
and now signified his conversion by taking out the false teeth
provided by Jemal the Great and stamping on them until
they were in fragments. British resources eventually provided
another set.

The striking force consisted of the 450-man Sherifian
Camel Corps, a small detachment of Egyptian Camel Corps
to carry out demolitions on the railway, Captain Pisani's French
mountain battery, a party of Gurkhas with four machine guns,
and two of the invaluable armored cars, bringing the total
strength of the force to some five thousand.

Meanwhile Jafar Pasha with the rest of the Arab Northern Army was directed to enter Ma'an should the Turks quit
it. Lawrence, detained by complex Arab politics, was late in
starting, but, driving with Lord Winterton, caught the regular column up before it reached Azraq. His companion, who
had been an M.P. almost as soon as he reached the year of full
manhood, was not an expert in Arab affairs, but was bursting
with enthusiasm and was then, as until his death in 1962, a
most likable character.

The move was completed on September 12. It was decided

not to attack Dera immediately because the RAF was unable to provide the necessary support and the garrison had been reinforced by German troops. Actual operations began on September 16, when the rail line was extensively destroyed north of the town. Lawrence, Winterton, and a third officer dealt with the other section to the south. The demolition was, Lawrence said, "a fine example of that finest sort which left the skeleton of its bridge intact, but tottering, so that the repairing enemy had a first labour to destroy the wreck, before they could attempt to rebuild."[4] On September 19 Captain F. G. Peake's Egyptians cut the railway halfway between Amman and Dera after a first failure when they encountered Bedouin defending it as Turkish hirelings. Meanwhile Nuri Bey and the Rualla tribesmen had moved northwest and had, also on September 19, cut the northern branch halfway between Dera and Samakh. Nuri was the life and soul of the party at this time. This good Moslem carried a large flask of whisky, the contents of which he shared generously.

The Arabs were not in any danger on the ground because the Turks had virtually no cavalry in this region and were far less mobile afoot. From the air was another matter. One of the two British aircraft had been put out of action, and the other, of the type used on the western front for photography, could not cope with the German fighters. Returning to Azraq, Lawrence took the aircraft which had carried the news of the British victory, landed at Ramle, and drove straight to GHQ. He explained his air problem to Allenby, who telephoned to Salmond, who in his turn promised to send two Bristol fighters, capable of dealing with any German aircraft. Salmond and Borton also agreed to load Ross Smith's Handley-Page with fuel, since there was none on the spot. Ross Smith flew in a Bristol to see if the giant aircraft could land.[5]

Meanwhile the Arabs had drawn back to a new camp to avoid the bombing and the fire of a German railway gun, but the Germans quickly discovered their removal on the morning of September 22. All now went well: two German aircraft were shot down, and Ross Smith, having ascertained that a landing with the big aircraft was not too difficult, flew back to bring over the Handley-Page. Finally, on September 27, the Turks set fire to their remaining six aircraft at Dera.

Lawrence flew to Azraq and brought back the Emir Feisal and Nuri esh Shalaan in a car, to find the Handley-Page unloading amid a crowd of Arab spectators who called it "*The* aeroplane" and the fighters its foals. Within two days railway movement had completely ceased, but on September 26 Colonel von Oppen brought his Asia Corps into Dera, repaired breaches in the rail line to Riyaq, and entrained for the junction.[6] This was the day on which Liman directed that the front should be re-formed from a point 26 miles south of Damascus on to Riyaq.

Meanwhile, Samakh had been stormed and Amman secured. The road to Damascus was open and only minor opposition was to be expected from wornout rear guards. "Before the astonished eyes of the Arabs the Turkish Syrian Empire was tumbling down. They saw their old enemy reeling to destruction; they saw a vision of freedom and, nearer at hand, a vision of loot. Their passion for both flamed up and possessed them."[7]

So far Nuri esh Shalaan had not been allowed to bring up his braves from Azraq because it was doubtful whether they would not clash with the fellahin. Now that there was prospect of loot from the enemy this consideration no longer obtained, and Feisal directed that they should march. At this time Lawrence was at odds with one of his best British officers, who took the view that the Arabs had done their job, that they were incapable of storming Dera by reason of their inadequate armament and a discipline extending only to their relatively small regular element, and that they should await the arrival of British troops. These reasons for inaction were cogent, but keen as Lawrence was on victories at small cost, bloodless for preference, they did not appeal to him. In any case he knew that Allenby wanted the place taken as early as possible.

Lawrence was loyal to his commander-in-chief, but there was one respect in which his allegiance and candor were incomplete: he hid from Allenby his soaring hopes for the Arab future. He knew of the Sykes-Picot Agreement and burned with shame when he reflected on this pledge to establish French rule in Syria. He was determined to reach Damascus with the vanguard, determined that the Arabs should play a part in its capture, determined that Feisal should be set up as ruler. He was prepared to balk the French at every point, and Colonel Brémond knew it. Lawrence had always disliked them, and now his sentiments amounted to hatred.[8] As regards the military situation he was right and the officer who thought the Arabs would fail to take Dera wrong, but the latter was not merely being a timid pessimist when he had pointed out the risk of a handful of slow-footed regulars being squeezed between the Turkish forces in the area and the Fourth Army moving northward.[9]

Of course Lawrence had his way. The column made a forced march northward and as it crossed the railway undid Colonel von Oppen's work by cutting the line once more. Beyond the breach Auda Abu Tayi left the line of march and captured a train. In twenty-four hours ending at noon on September 27 some two thousand prisoners were taken, including a number of Germans and a handful of Austrians. Finally the Arabs broke into Dera, which the main body of the Turks had abandoned, leaving only a rear guard behind, and took it without difficulty. They spent the night of September 27 slaughtering and burning. Being the junction point for all the railways to the south, Dera always contained large quantities of food and ammunition, which provided splendid plunder. On the following morning the first contact was made with General Barrow's 4th Cavalry Division. The situation of the retreating enemy was now deplorable.

"Some units had got through by train and were thus beyond reach of pursuit. But the greater number, already exhausted by forced marches, by lack of food and sleep, with hearts broken by dread of mounted pursuit and of the yet swifter enemy in the skies above, with boots worn to ribbons, had about seventy-five miles to cover before they could reach the city."[10]

Presently an aircraft crossed the Arabs' line of march and dropped a message to the effect that two bodies of Turks —the smaller from a point near the railway six miles northeast, the bigger, some six thousand, from Dera—were moving north. Lawrence decided, in view of the fact that the 4th Cavalry Division's advanced guard was still some miles short of the town, to tackle the smaller force first, particularly because it was heading for Talal's community at Tafas. He went forward, with nothing but his personal bodyguard, to delay the Turks till the regular forces reached the scene. He was too late to avert the tragedy at Tafas, though with the aid of the indefatigable Pisani, who brought up his mountain guns at top speed, the Turkish column was forced to veer northeastward, so that Lawrence, Auda Abu Tayi, and Talal were able to enter the village behind it. There he found that the Turks could slaughter with a savagery far worse than the Arabs, who rarely, if ever, killed women and children.

A little child ran from Lawrence in terror crying out: "Don't hit me, Baba!" It then fell to the ground with blood pouring from a mortal wound. They found, too, dead women disgustingly mutilated. Of one woman Lawrence writes: "I looked close and saw the body of a woman folded across it [a sheep hurdle], bottom upwards, nailed there by a saw bayonet the hilt of which stuck hideously in the air between her naked legs."[11] Talal pulled his headcloth over his head and rode at the Turks, to be immediately shot dead. Auda called to Allah for mercy on Talal's soul and swore that the Turks should pay the price.

Lawrence harried the small column till it finally split into three groups, two of which he finally destroyed. The third group, all German, resisted unflinchingly. Time after time it halted long enough to beat off an attack, then resumed its formation, as Lawrence puts it, "sheering through the wrack of Turk and Arab like armoured ships, high-faced and silent." He admired this resistance intensely. However, an order was issued that there was to be no quarter. Every prisoner was killed, and the heads of the wounded were bashed in. His French biographer is here kinder to Lawrence than his best English biographer. Liddell Hart remarks that after the Turkish atrocities his order to spare none was superfluous. But was this his personal order, as he says? At all events, Beraud-Villars points out that Lawrence did later make an effort to dissuade the Bedouin from murdering one batch of prisoners.[12]

Meanwhile the greater column had not been left unmolested. The Arabs had clung like leeches and prevented it from camping for the night. It, too, was becoming disorganized, splitting like the other column, and dropping stragglers who had become completely exhausted. But Lawrence was looking ahead. He did not desire that the Bedouin should become as exhausted as the Turks, since they would be required for a more serious task if more Turkish columns appeared from the south. Accordingly, he rode out on a camel in the darkness, came up with the Rualla and, after some argument, withdrew them from the hunt. On returning to camp, he found that the blood feuds so characteristic of the tribes were reappearing and that peace had been imperiled; indeed, but for the capture of Dera, it might not have been possible to maintain it.[13] The situation had eased when word came that Dera had been taken. It was just as well. When bigotry and lust for slaughter are stirred up there is no telling how far they will go. Lawrence set out once more with Nuri Bey, but this time he rode his famed she-camel Baha, "the great rebellious Baha," outdistanced the others, and rode into Dera alone at dawn.

Lawrence put guards on the engines and pumps, and took some measures to restore order and stop the killing of such Turks as had remained. He had certain of the instincts and address of a military administrator, as he was to show at Damascus, but on this occasion he had a spur unusually great. The 4th Cavalry Division was at hand; unaware that Dera had fallen, it was preparing to take the place. Lawrence was eager to prove that his irregular Arab troops could restore and maintain discipline of a standard approximating that of which regulars were capable. Before setting out to meet the divisional commander he shaved, put on clean robes, and determined to behave with "histrionic nonchalance." The leading troops of the 4th Cavalry Division held him up for some time, unable to decide on his credentials and thinking he might be a spy, but he met Barrow at last. According to his own account, he found General Barrow nonplussed by having been beaten to the goal—a sentiment which, if true, must have been accentuated when Lawrence told Barrow blandly that Barrow's men would be the guest of the Arabs, and still more so when Barrow was informed that there was no need to post sentries because that had been done.

All this did not, however, cause Barrow to lose his good manners. Catching sight of a pennon in front of the building formerly occupied by the Turkish camp commandant and now the office of Sherif Nasir, almost the last notable of the Hejaz who had accompanied Feisal 750 miles northward, General Barrow saluted it, to the intense delight of the watching Arabs.

PURSUIT TO DAMASCUS

8 ALLENBY AT TIMES could be taciturn indeed. Through-out the operations described he had breathed not a word, even to Chauvel, that he contemplated an expansion of his plan. Just as in 1917 he had said nothing to indicate to Bulfin that he contemplated a wheel out of the coast plain to take Jeru-salem. On that occasion, however, Allenby had been ordered to secure the Holy City, whereas now he had been given no strategic objectives, except that in December 1917 he had been directed to clear Palestine "from Dan to Beersheba." This was typical Lloyd Georgian imprecision, and the precise Allenby had answered that he accepted the task, "understanding Dan to be about Baniyas."[1] It was, however, agreed that he should try to drive Turkey out of the war.

Allenby's first mention of Damascus was on September 22, but the offensive had not then succeeded in breaking the hostile rear guards. On September 26 he held a corps com-manders' conference as a prelude to his orders for the advance. On the same day he relieved the pressure on his administrative staff by handing over control of the country south of a line drawn from the Nahr el Faliq to the coast to the Inspector General, Lines of Communication. The advance on Damascus was to be carried out by the Desert Mounted Corps under

General Chauvel, and that on Beirut, where little resistance
was expected, by the XXI Corps. Two divisions of the Desert
Mounted Corps were to move west of the Sea of Galilee, the
third division would move west of the railway.

The problem was now simplified. The two Turkish armies
in Palestine had been destroyed. The Turkish Fourth Army,
though unbroken, had suffered heavy loss and seemed unlikely
to reach Damascus ahead of the British cavalry. Allenby's sole
worry was whether the transport, including some taken over
from the XXI Corps, would be able to keep up. As it turned
out, a major proportion of the transport did fail, but fortunately the cavalry was able to requisition food for man and
beast on the road.[2] The British railway was being carried
forward toward Tul Karm on the Turkish permanent way, but
did not reach there until October 15.

There is no better tonic than the scent of victory, and the
whole Desert Mounted Corps was now at the top of its form.
The Australian Mounted Division, united for the first time,
quitted Tiberias early on September 27, men and horses
freshened by their brief rest by the Sea of Galilee. The 5th
Cavalry Division followed close behind. The famous old bridge
of Jisr Benat Yakub over the Jordan had been cut but not
destroyed, and the enemy held the far bank under the gallant
defender of Samakh, Captain von Keyserling.[3] Major-General
Hodgson directed Brigadier-General Wilson to look for fords
with his 3rd Brigade, but Wilson could not reach the far
bank until he had been reinforced by the other two brigades.
The establishment of a bridgehead made things no easier in
daylight and he was repeatedly checked during the day, but
he got the 10th Regiment over in the dusk.[4] A squadron overran a small post which defended gallantly, capturing 12 Germans, 40 Turks, and 3 guns.[5]

Meanwhile the Corps Bridging Train had put up a trestle
to span the demolished arch at Jisr Benat Yakub. The head of
the division reached Quneitra at 1 P.M. and found abundant
water—so abundant that the whole division could bivouac
there, less the 3rd Brigade, which pushed on a few miles north-

ward. Quneitra was a Circassian village, and in case the inhabitants gave trouble Chauvel decided to concentrate a strong force to cover his lines of communication. Two regiments of the 5th Cavalry Division were attached and this force was placed under the orders of Brigadier-General Grant.

On the morning of September 29 armored cars located a strong force astride the road southwest of Sasa. It was possibly an error on the part of Major-General Hodgson to stick to his order that the advance should not begin until afternoon. At all events it was found impossible to close with the enemy in face of registered machine-gun fire by daylight. Dismounted action was then tried and finally an attack guided by the flashes of the machine guns took all six guns without loss. The enemy made off in trucks, having succeeded in substantially delaying the advance. It was estimated that the enemy force numbered about fifteen hundred, three hundred of them Germans.

At 5 A.M. on September 30 the advance was resumed, and as dawn broke a small body of enemy troops was encountered. The Turks had four guns, but they did not fire because no one understood the gun mechanism.[6] The Turks and Germans alike fled in confusion, but some 350 prisoners were taken before the horses had to be rested. Just ahead lay the Nahr Barbar, once known as the Pharpar—as its twin, the Barada, is the ancient Abana.

Major-General Hodgson now gave his brigadiers their further orders. The 5th Light Horse Brigade was to advance at top speed on Damascus, while two regiments under the command of Lieutenant-Colonel M. W. J. Bourchier were to engage a Turkish column which had taken up a position with its right flank on Kaukab. The whole division now deployed, each brigade in column of squadrons in lines of troop columns. It has been much debated whether or not Allenby's cavalry was the last to perform a major exploit, but there is no question that this particular deployment has never been repeated. "The grey Barbs and Arabs, the picturesque uniforms of the Spahis and Chasseurs d'Afrique on the left front, added to the magnificence of the spectacle."[7] The French troops swung round

the Turkish flank as the Australians attacked frontally. This
time the Turks had no artillery, so that the two horse-artillery
batteries could engage at short range and the Light Horse
could charge. The Turks broke at once in wild flight, so fast
that, on the broken ground, it was impossible to overtake
them. It was the first occasion on which a German contingent
had panicked.

The enemy force numbered over five thousand, but its
fighting days were over. It reached the gorge of the Barada
safely, but the French climbed onto the higher ground up-
stream and headed it off. Turning back towards Damascus,
the Turkish force came under fire from a handful of Australians and promptly threw down their arms, 4,000 prisoners
being taken. The 3rd Brigade had been ordered to avoid
Damascus, but Wilson felt this to be impossible, since the
only link with the Homs road was through it. On Hodgson's
instructions he remained where he was for the night. The men
could sleep through anything, but some were kept awake by
the constant explosions of ammunition and fuel.

The 5th Cavalry Division in rear of the Australians had
been held up by the engagement at Sasa, where it arrived at
8:30 A.M. on September 30. A few minutes later Chauvel's
orders to intercept another column on the Pilgrims' Road
(Darb el Hajj) from Dera, at this point nine miles east of
the Quneitra road, reached Major-General Macandrew. He
ordered the leading brigade, followed by the Essex Battery,
to carry out the task, making as good a pace as it could across
country.

Brigadier-General G. V. Clarke was short a regiment of
the 14th Brigade because the Sherwood Rangers were at
Quneitra, but his two Indian regiments, the Deccan and Poona
Horse, had hardly been engaged as yet. Patrols presently returned to report that the Turks were holding the hills to the
north where the Australians had been engaged before going
through to Damascus. In the hills they held a pass through
which a compact column, six abreast and with a great deal

of transport, was moving on Damascus, while further north another body of troops could be observed nearing the city. The party, about 2,000 strong, at Kiswe kept up so hot a fire that it was out of the question to close.

Macandrew, whose sole weakness, if it were such, was that he could not wait in patience in a situation like this, had been worrying all night over the delay. He now sent Brigadier-General Clarke a message, directing him to neglect the hostile troops to the south and make straight for Damascus. The prospect of attacking a force of this strength with two regiments was hair-raising, and Clarke was very well pleased to get the new order. He dropped a squadron to keep the enemy force in Kiswe under observation and got his brigade on the move before noon. The Deccan Horse tried to charge the enemy three miles further north, but could not get to close quarters, so fast was his flight. It did, however, take 200 prisoners, including the commander of the Turkish 3rd Cavalry Division and all that remained of one of his brigades. This enemy division, which had been nearly useless for many months, had sadly stained its outstandingly high record in the Second and Third Battles of Gaza.

At 2:30 P.M. Macandrew ordered his 13th Cavalry Brigade to advance on Kiswe, but before it closed on the place Chauvel arrived at Kaukab and canceled the order because he considered that the force in the village was doomed anyhow. Meanwhile Major M. D. Vigors, with a squadron of Hodson's Horse, had been pursuing a small body of Turks, who halted after first falling back. Vigors began a charge, but the Turks at once put up their hands. Immediately after, Hodson's Horse won another triumph: Risaldar Nur Ahmed rode forward, at first accompanied only by his orderly, right into the streets of Kiswe. After he had shot one man, almost 300 surrendered.

At about the same time Major Vigors caught sight of a large body of the enemy, which he estimated at fifteen hundred. His urgent message demanding reinforcement went astray and he had had to employ two troops to escort rearwards the prisoners already in his hands. Obviously he could effect nothing with the strength remaining, but not knowing that his mounted messenger had been temporarily knocked out, he had every reason to suppose that the whole brigade would attack the Turkish flank while he checked the movement northward. As things were, he lost some horses and had to abandon a Hotchkiss light machine gun, but was lucky enough otherwise to bring the troop off without a scratch.

Half an hour earlier Captain Lord Apsley had made a determined effort to save the neighboring Turkish wireless station from destruction. As his troop of the Gloucester Hussars and Hotchkiss machine-gun section advanced, the radio mast was seen to fall amidst thick smoke. At closer quarters it became clear that both the wireless station and the railway station were in flames. Local villagers now told him that the enemy demolition parties numbered five hundred. Still he would not call it a day. He led two successful charges, killing a number of Turks and Germans and moving in so close that he could see with his own eyes there was nothing left to save.

The Fourth Cavalry Division was left at the point where its leading troops had made contact with the enemy west of Dera. On the morning of September 26 the 10th Cavalry Brigade, detached at Jisr el Majami, marched on Irbid, a village halfway between the Jordan and Dera. The distance was over twenty miles on a wretched and stony track, so that undue speed would have involved cut fetlocks or pasterns. The one regiment which occasionally trotted in the later stages was the 2nd Lancers, ordered to reach Irbid in daylight if possible. A mile and a half short of Irbid a narrow defile, fortunately not held, was passed; but, on moving out of it, fire was opened from a plateau beyond. Since darkness was approaching and the brigade would have to halt for the night without water unless Irbid was at once secured, the commanding officer, Major G. Gould—who had succeeded the redoubtable Captain Davison three days earlier—determined to attack at once. He ordered one squadron to bypass the village on the northern side and attack it from the east, a second to attack it from the north, and a third from the south.

The first squadron met with such hot machine-gun fire that it was stopped dead about a thousand yards north of Irbid. The second squadron came under equally heavy fire, whereupon the squadron leader swung slightly right to enter the village at the northwest corner, but to his dismay saw one troop keep straight on, to be shot down almost to a man. His own following had also suffered, so that he was left with only eight men. There was nothing to be done but get out, and he himself was lucky to survive, having been thrice wounded. The third squadron made a fatal mistake in taking for Irbid a smaller village three-quarters of a mile to the northwest.

Brigadier-General Green, who arrived on the scene immediately after the start of the attack, was anxious to get the Berks Battery into action, but it was blocked by the Central India Horse in the defile and did not open fire in time to support the lancers. As the Central India Horse, having dropped a squadron southwest of Irbid, reached the plateau, an orderly from the brigadier rode up and gave the verbal message: "Your orders are to follow the squadron of the 2nd Lancers down the valley."

British cavalry officers, above all others, ought to take to heart the lesson of Balaclava that a vague order should be confirmed if possible. On this occasion it would have been easier for Major J. R. Hutchinson to refer to Green than it had been for Lucan to refer to Raglan, but Hutchinson decided not to take this course because the light was already failing. Actually Green had not meant that the regiment should confine itself to the valley. Hutchinson formed squadron columns and led the regiment forward at a gallop. His C Squadron saw C Squadron of the lancers, which it had been directed to support, and followed its error, thus being able to exert no influence in the action. His A Squadron switched away from the machine-gun fire and took refuge in the hollow ground west of Irbid. Major Hutchinson managed to stop D Squadron. Meanwhile his B Squadron to the south charged through the tiny hamlet of Zabda, a mile and a half southwest of Irbid, and pressed on to cut the Dera road to the east, but was held up. Had there been a German contingent in the defending force losses would have been grave, but the Turkish marksmanship was extremely erratic. The casualties in men numbered only forty-six, the great majority in the 2nd Lancers, but those in horses, which are unrecorded, must have been considerably higher.[8]

This incident has been recorded in detail because it was the only defeat suffered by Allenby's cavalry, far more a defeat than the check incurred at Aleppo only five days before the conclusion of the armistice with Turkey. The affair bristles with lessons. First of all, there had been no reconnaissance. The reason for this was lack of time, but how lucky was the brigade to pay such a relatively small price! Next day, when Irbid was found empty, it was learned from the villagers that the Turks had numbered some five thousand, that they belonged to the Fourth Army, and that they had suffered no defeat. Either Green had sent an inadequate order, or the orderly deformed it, or the recipient misinterpreted it. The record of victories won by extreme boldness proved heady wine. Finally, the brigade staff spent much of the night coding a message to be sent by wireless, describing the situation at great length, which took equally long to decode at divisional headquarters. Parts of it might well have been sent in the clear, but even if this had been thought inadvisable some time would have been saved by sending it in sections, a rudimentary practice.

Barrow, at Jisr el Majami with his 11th Brigade, had thus no news of the 10th Brigade till the morning, but he sent an order which reached it before dawn to march in the direction of Dera. He directed the 12th Brigade, in bivouac a little east of the Jordan, to move at 6 A.M. and join the 10th Brigade. Green's third regiment, the Dorset Yeomanry, had not been engaged in the action and was fresh. Moving as advanced guard, this time by a good road, the Dorsets approached Er Remta, seven miles short of Dera, and learned from a message dropped from the air that it was unoccupied. Lieutenant-Colonel G. K. M. Mason fortunately did not neglect precautions, but ordered a reconnaissance. The leading troops came under heavy machine-gun fire, withdrew to cover, and dismounted. At once an enemy force of three hundred emerged from the village, the greater part of them halting on a good position and setting up four machine guns, while the remainder boldly attacked. Three of Mason's troops swept into the Turkish left flank and destroyed this smaller party. Then the Yeomanry penetrated Er Remta, dismounted and speedily cleared it.

Green had ordered a squadron of the Central India Horse to support the Dorsets and the remainder of the regiment to push on and intercept the Turks reported to be heading for Dera. The regiment came up with them speedily and by an instant attack took them by surprise, capturing about half of them and their four machine guns. Then the third squadron caught up with yet another party, overran it, and took some 90 prisoners and another four machine guns. Though the afternoon was still before him, Barrow, arriving on the scene, ordered the brigade to bivouac. He has been accused of "a reaction to excessive caution," and it is pointed out that he missed the chance of heading off the Turkish Fourth Army, which was a day out of Dera when he arrived there on September 28. This criticism is unfair and fails to bring out the point that he would probably have foundered a large number of horses had he pressed on.[9] He ordered the 10th Brigade to send out patrols at first light to find out whether Dera was still in the enemy's hands.

Next morning, these patrols caught sight of flames rising from the station and saw that the hospital roof had collapsed. About 7 A.M. Green met Lawrence and learned that the place had been entered by the Arabs the previous day. Lawrence then went back westward to find Barrow, and the divisional commander rode into Dera. Barrow realized that he could hardly overtake and capture the main body of the Fourth Army alone; so he requested Chauvel to detach a force from the road followed by the Australian Mounted Division to head off the enemy. Unhappily, the delay in crossing the Jordan at Jisr Benat Yakub rendered this impossible.[10]

Now follows the clash between Barrow and Lawrence, on which a great deal of ink has been expended. Lawrence tells us that Barrow was "dazed at my calm assumption that he was my guest," which is understandable![11] Lawrence also makes some fantastic comments on the Indian regiments and on the relations between the British officers and the other ranks, which the affection of Indian troops for their leaders —and, indeed, the present-day affection of the Indian and Pakistani armies for their memory—belies. Nutting is doubtless right in saying that Lawrence behaved "with a typical mixture of schoolboy impudence and omniscient superiority," but, if he had known Barrow, a gay, smiling, little man, he would not have described him as "a stiff professional soldier,"[12] though it may be confessed that for the rest of his life he never had a good word for Lawrence. It is also fair to point out that Lawrence was sickened and overwrought by the sights at Tafas. Wavell, a great admirer of Lawrence's—indeed of all unorthodox fighters—and the supporter to an imprudent degree of "the Lawrence of the Second World War," Orde Wingate, condemns his attitude to Barrow.[13]

What, however, had turned Barrow's stomach was the spectacle before him. He has said himself that in all his service in this war he had never seen such appalling misery. As the official history puts it, "the sight of Deraa Station and its encampments that met the 10th Cavalry Brigade as it rode in that morning was ghastly beyond aught that any man had yet witnessed. Everywhere there were dead Turks, but they were the fortunate ones; for the wounded lay scattered about, despoiled and in agony, amid a litter of packages, half-looted, half burnt, of torn documents, and smashed machinery. A hospital train stood in the station; the driver and fireman were still in their cab, still alive, but mortally wounded; the sick and wounded in the train had been stripped of every rag of clothing".[14]

Barrow got on much better with the amiable Nuri Bey,

and it was with him that he arranged for the Arabs to cover his march on the following day. To the 10th Brigade he allotted a work of mercy, that of dressing the Turkish wounded. They also buried the dead and cleared up the mess as far as possible before they lay down to rest. The other two brigades moved for the night to Mezerib, eleven miles to the northwest, because there was not water enough for them at Dera.

On the morning of September 29 these brigades and the divisional troops marched up the Pilgrims' Road, to halt in the early afternoon thirteen miles northeast of Mezerib, where they were joined by the 10th Brigade, less a squadron dropped at Dera to guard the wounded and such rolling stock as had not been set afire. The division was for the first time short of food and forage. At Irbid had been found a fair quantity of barley and a little herd of cattle, sheep, and goats, which the division had brought on on the hoof, and at Dera more goats for the Hindu troops and fodder for the horses. On leaving Mezerib only thirteen wagons of the divisional train were full, and not till Damascus was reached could the division dispense with requisitioning, the results of which were moderately rewarding. A few wounded men were carried forward by the field ambulances, and a number of sick Turks, with the result that influenza patients had to ride their horses all the way. Many sick Turks had to be abandoned to the Bedouin and fellahin.

On September 30 the division marched for Kiswe, but on the route Barrow decided that thirty miles was too far for the horses and gave the order to halt for the night. Hardly had this been carried out when Lawrence appeared to inform Brigadier-General Gregory, commanding the 11th Cavalry Brigade, that the stronger of two Turkish forces—which, it will be recalled, the Arabs had decided to neglect while they annihilated the lesser—should now be dealt with, and demanded his aid. Lawrence had at last found a cavalry leader whom he could admire and is enthusiastic about Gregory's "happy vigour."[15] Gregory sent forward the Hants Battery at top speed, and firing over open sights, though outranged by

the enemy's German-made mountain guns, the battery com-
pelled the column to veer away. Lawrence certainly exag-
gerates in declaring that the enemy column was practically
destroyed by Auda during the night, since it was still fifteen to
sixteen hundred strong when cut off, as will appear, by the
Australians on October 2. (It was this column that was engaged by Vigors on September 30. He then estimated it at
fifteen hundred, but might easily have erred in this, since he
had not the strength to close.) At all events, Auda did a big
killing and afterwards relented enough to take prisoners. Many
hundreds of dead were later found by British patrols.

The Arab-born commander at Damascus, a grey-haired
veteran in the Turkish service, had been reorganizing the
artillery, and the British soon learned how he had done it.
During the afternoon of September 30, having seen Jemal
Pasha depart for the north, he deserted to the British, leaving
the city at a gallop and riding straight to the headquarters
of the 4th Cavalry Division. Breakfasting at 2 A.M. on October
1 with Barrow, General Ali Riza Pasha el Rikabi laughed so
heartily over the story of how he had ordered the heavy
batteries to positions where they could not be served for lack
of water that he kicked over the table in the darkness and
spilt the scrambled eggs and cocoa. Barrow used to say after
the war: "We had plenty of both, so we did not worry, and
within ten minutes we were all enjoying our early breakfast."

In no case could there be a serious defense of Damascus.
There never has been in its history. It is in no sense a fortress,
and if its possessors were defeated outside it was always captured and generally sacked.

"If Jerusalem is a city of soldiers and priests, Damascus
is a city of merchants and shopkeepers. . . . The site of Damascus was determined by the movement of trade as surely as
were those of Venice and Marseilles; it is a port of the desert
as they are ports of the sea. The city lies on a plateau between
desert and mountain, upon the most important trade route
between Syria and Mesopotamia, and therefore, over long
periods, between Europe and Asia. . . . This site was the nat-

ural port and depot for the merchant navigators of the desert
—the nomad tribes—steering whether from Babylon or Baghdad. A halting place, a place of exchange or bazaar, a settlement, a city: such were the stages in the growth of Damascus
—stages of very long ago, for it has some claim to be the
oldest inhabited city known to man."[16]

The city awaited its latest conquerors in a state of mingled
turmoil, dread, and delighted expectation. Even before the
departure of Liman, crowds of Bedouin had been galloping
through the streets, firing their rifles in the air, but doing no
great harm. These were not the most irregular of the Sherifian
irregulars but local men, though they wished Feisal well and
raised his flag over the Town Hall. The Turks in passage
through did not venture to pull it down. After darkness, when
the Barada Gorge had been sealed, there was virtually an end
to this exodus. A handful took the very bad road to Homs,
but the vast majority resigned themselves to capture and remained.

The dread and delighted expectation were shared by the
large Christian community, a fifth of the citizens, roughly
60,000 out of 300,000.[17] Much as they hated the Turks, they
had at this moment more reason to fear the Arabs and prayed
that the British would outdistance them. The Christian Syrians
had another reason for this sentiment: they firmly believed
that Britain and her allies would give them an independent
state, whereas the Arabs were counting on Britain to give them
dominion from the southern limits of the Hejaz to the foot
of the Taurus, a distance of 1,250 miles. Alas for their hopes!
They were to be belied by British commitments, French ambitions, and, where the Arabs were concerned, by their in-
ternecine feuds.

Lawrence had passed an uneasy night. He had lain down
in his blanket on the hard ground, but before he obtained
much needed sleep he heard tremendous explosions and saw
a glare above the city.

Raising himself on his elbows, Lawrence exclaimed: "Good

God! They are burning the town!" He felt sick at the thought
that this goal of their endeavors might be reduced to ashes at
the moment of its freedom—yet to Stirling he showed no
other trace of emotion and merely said: "Anyhow, I've sent
Rualla forward, and we should soon have four thousand men
in and around the town."[18]

The noise and glare had come, in fact, from the destruction of the ammunition and stores by German engineers before leaving Damascus. As Lawrence caught sight of the city
his fears were relieved and he saw it like "a pearl in the
morning sun." Further on he met a horseman who shouted:
"Good news! Damascus salutes you." It was the messenger
sent by Shruki, who had temporarily succeeded Ali Riza
Pasha. Lawrence sent back word to Sherif Nasir to join him
and then sent Nasir on to enter the city first, with the excuse
that he himself needed to wash and shave. Then he followed,
to witness the scenes of wild excitement.

Brigadier-General Wilson had only the haziest notion of
what might be happening in Damascus when his 3rd Light
Horse Brigade began its advance at 5 A.M. The advanced guard
crossed the Barada, but was then held up because the road
was blocked by wagons, dead bodies, and the carcasses of
animals, including a flock of sheep caught by machine-gun
fire during the night. One squadron took three-quarters of an
hour clearing these obstacles so that the advanced guard could
continue. Coming out of the gorge, Major A. C. N. Olden,
second-in-command of the 10th Light Horse Brigade, ordered
the leading squadron to enter the city at a gallop. The 10th
Light Horse Brigade rode in before 6:30 A.M.[19] Australians
and Arabs both claim to have entered first, but the issue remains undecided. Some of the irregulars certainly rode in
before midnight on September 30, but they dared not attack
the Turks, who, for their part, could not distinguish them
from the local Bedouin who had long been demonstrating.

The gallop of the Australians could not long be maintained
because the streets were full of delighted men. Women leaned
out of windows to drop rose leaves, scent, and confetti on

their heads. "Covered with dust, the horsemen showed no sign of excitement or even gratification," though "they missed no dark smiling eyes at the windows."[20] By 7 A.M. Wilson was clear of the city. Meanwhile Macandrew had gone forward with the 14th Cavalry Brigade, and rode in at 10:30 A.M. Coming from the south, he and his troops were also accorded a welcome as enthusiastic as was given the Australians by the people of this quarter. Once more Damascus had been yielded without defense.

TRAGEDY IN DAMASCUS

9 THE PERIOD OF REJOICING in Damascus was brief. Within a matter of hours all but the most callous of the conquerors whose duties kept them in the city were deeply depressed by the scenes they witnessed. These scenes of bloodshed and violence lasted until the triumphal march through the city, headed by Chauvel and his three divisional commanders, Barrow, Macandrew, and Hodgson, with representatives of their staffs, on October 2. The troops were a squadron of each regiment, a battery from each division, a section of the 2nd New Zealand Machine-gun Squadron, and a squadron of the 2nd Light Horse Brigade from the Australian and New Zealand Mounted Division, the last-named acting as Chauvel's bodyguard. The 3rd Light Horse Brigade, now engaged far from the city, was the only unit of the Desert Mounted Corps not represented. This procession had a great moral effect on the onlookers, as it was meant to. Violence came to an abrupt end and Damascus returned to work, so far as that was possible, and to its natural occupation, trade.

Here we must glance at the development of Damascus politics. A considerable power, not only in Damascus but also in all northern Syria, was represented by immigrants whose elder generation had escaped or been deported by the French from Algeria after its conquest. At their head were two brothers, the elder of whom carried immense prestige because he bore the name of Abd el Kader, who had so heroically defended his country. Lawrence had encountered him and his brother Mohammed Said before, and more than suspected them of treachery to the Arab cause, which was true in the sense that they were playing for their own hand.

When Lawrence reached the anteroom of the Town Hall he found the younger brother proclaiming his right to leadership. To deal with him was a pressing task, but Lawrence had to put it aside while he separated Auda Abu Tayi and Sultan el Atrash, chief of the Druses, whose dealings with Liman have already been described and who had, four days after his first meeting with him on September 21, taken bribes not to molest his troops in their retreat. This diversion being over and the Algerians having gone out for refreshment with Sherif Nasir, Lawrence took his own candidate, Shukri Pasha, out to show himself on a tour of the city and then returned to the Town Hall.[1]

Abd el Kader and Mohammed Said were not back, and when Lawrence sent for them the reply came that they were asleep. He told another Druse that if they did not appear he would send British troops to seek them out. The bluff, for such it clearly was, worked. The attitude of Nuri esh Shalaan was still somewhat doubtful, but on learning that though the English were sure to come, they might never go, he pledged the support of the Rualla. Next the two Algerians returned with a well-armed escort, but on seeing themselves out-numbered hesitated whether to fight or parley. Lawrence at once declared the governorship of Mohammed Said dissolved, owing to their hostility to Feisal, and in Feisal's name appointed Shukri Pasha acting military governor. Abd el Kader was so infuriated that he drew his dagger, but again Auda was on the watch and jumped forward so menacingly in defense of Lawrence that the aggressor stepped back and quitted the room with his brother. Lawrence then turned to business, and he was a good businessman, though his part thereafter is exaggerated by himself and by several of his English devotees who have written about him, but not by one able French writer who praises his work here.[2] To begin with, he was clever enough to make use of the officials who had served the Turks, to the detriment of Feisal's adherents. As things were, the first Arab administration broke down within a few days, Shukri resigned, and Ali Riza Pasha el Rikabi succeeded him as military governor.[3]

Late in the first night in Damascus Lawrence heard a muezzin, who "with a ringing voice of special sweetness, cried into my window from a near mosque . . . 'God alone is great: I testify there are no gods but God, and Mohammed is his prophet. Come to prayer, come to security. God alone is great: there is no god—but God.'

"At the close he dropped his voice two tones, almost to speaking level, and softly added: 'And he is very good to us this day, O people of Damascus.' The clamour hushed as everyone seemed to obey the call to prayer on this their first night of perfect freedom."[4]

Lawrence's most difficult problems were bound up with the Sykes-Picot Agreement. Under the terms of this pact, already known to King Hussein and his sons, Syria and Mesopotamia had been divided into four zones: "A," "B," "Blue," and "Red." "A" and "Blue" were both to be French "spheres of influence"—by no means "colonies"—but were to be set up on very different terms. "Blue" covered Syria north of Acre and west of Damascus and Aleppo. Here the French were to establish an administration in consultation with a future Arab state or confederacy, but in "A" they were pledged to the support of an *independent* Arab state, a triangle from Aleppo, down to the Sea of Galilee, and over the desert to Rowanduz, a town in Kurdistan, taking in Aleppo, Homs, and Damascus. Allenby naturally permitted the French to take over "Blue," with a capital at largely French-speaking Beirut, as soon as the military situation made this feasible, but he insisted that in "A" they should recognize the authority of the Arabs, just as the British would in "B," east of the Jordan Valley. The eastern limit of this zone was not defined and could not be, owing to the power of Ibn Saud—who was friendly to the British but hostile to King Hussein—and Ibn Rashid, Emir of Hail—who had been a useful Turkish ally but had dropped in value, being suspected by them of an intention to change sides, and confined as hostage for the good behavior of his Shammar tribesmen.[5] Allenby would have erred gravely had he allowed the French to establish themselves in Damascus. What he did arrange was that, should the Arabs seek advice from European officials, these should be French in "A" and British in "B." On October 3 Allenby met Feisal and informed him that he was prepared to recognize an Arab administration of enemy territory east of the Jordan, from Ma'an to Damascus inclusive. He also said that he was appointing two liaison officers, British and French, to communicate with him through his chief political officer about the affairs of the Arab administration.

A few days before the signature of the Mudros Armistice on October 31 Allenby informed the British War Office of his new arrangements for the military administration of Syrian and Palestinian territory already occupied or likely to be. For his immediate purposes he was obliged to vary to some extent the application of the Sykes-Picot Agreement. There were now to be three areas: Occupied Enemy Territory South, North, and East. The first two comprised respectively the "Red" and "Blue" zones of the treaty, the third such portions of "A" and "B" as had come under Allenby's control. In "South"—the former "Red"—he already had an administration of this kind, that of country occupied in 1917, and he now placed the chief administrator, Major-General Sir A. W. Money, in control of all Palestine. "North" came under the Frenchman, Colonel de Piépape, and "East" under General Ali Pasha el Rikabi, who held his Governorship in Damascus but a short time.

Allenby felt obliged to restrict Occupied Enemy Territory North for convenience of administration and still more for moral reasons. "Since the signature of the Sykes-Picot Agreement a great wave of what may be described as democratic nationalism had swept over the Old World. The entry of America into the war and the collapse of Russia had both helped to raise it, but it sprang from a deep-seated sentiment in the bosoms of oppressed nations which diplomacy could not ignore, and which British diplomacy, at least, did not desire to ignore. This sentiment had a very important effect on the political situation in the Middle East, in that it seemed to clash with the provisions of the Sykes-Picot Agreement. Its force was recognized by both France and Britain in a declaration dated November 7th . . . for transmission to King Hussein and for circulation in the native press."[6]

This declaration began with the statement that the goal of the two powers was the complete freedom of peoples oppressed by the Turks and the establishment of more democratic forms of government. The two nations had therefore agreed on the establishment of administrations in Syria and Mesopotamia and their full recognition as soon as they were well established. Their sole care would be to secure the normal and effective working of these. The United Kingdom had no political interests in the country—though keeping an eye on Southern Palestine as a valuable air link with India and the Far East—but France had. Britain was not hostile to French ambitions, but she was nervous about them. The precautions she could take were temporary only. If France insisted on her pound of flesh she must have it. Unhappily she did so at Versailles, with disastrous consequences. Britain did her utmost to save something from the wreck and it will be shown that her efforts were largely successful. Where she had erred was in the Sykes-Picot Agreement itself.

"The Government could legitimately support the interest of France in Syria, where her scholars, her doctors, her traders, and her monks had accomplished honourable work. It could reasonably make an offer to Jews calculated to rally to its cause the power of international Jewry. But to hand

negotiations, as happened, to different representatives aware
only of the pledges they themselves were giving was unworthy
of the traditions of the country."[7]

Lawrence was given admirable support in his hasty
reorganization by Colonel Nuri Bey. His first care was
naturally the restoration of a supply of pure water. The streets
were cleared of filth; the electric lighting and the telegraph
were got going; the fires were extinguished. Fresh bank-
notes were run off the press and maximum prices fixed. Since in
the Turkish possessions a measure such as this could never be
made wholly effective, it may easily be realized that it was
still less so in these times of unrest, but it was at least a step
in the right direction. Nuri Bey cleared the streets of looters
and rioters by drastic methods, and henceforth property
became relatively safe, without the Desert Mounted Corps
being required to maintain law and order more than occasionally.

The great task, however, was to deal with the many
thousands of sick Turks. Here, though Lawrence made a
start, the work of mercy fell mainly on the British Royal
Army Medical Corps and the Australian Army Medical Corps.
Magnificent work was, however, performed by Australian
combatant officers in succoring the diseased, the broken-down,
and the wounded. Nearly all the diseases known to man were
prevalent, with the happy exception of the worst of all,
cholera. This had been kept at bay by Falkenhayn's chief
medical officer, Obergeneralarzt Steuber, who had isolated
every unit which had the disease in its ranks. Only a single
British soldier caught it and Tiberias was the only town
where a few civilians were affected. Its twin sister, typhus,
was now rife.* Ophthalmia, a disease of the country—the
one-eyed Wavell had been urged by colleagues not to come
out for this reason—was prevalent among the captives, as

---

* English translators constantly give a false impression by rendering
the German *Typhus* as "typhus." *Typhus* means typhoid fever; *Fleck-
typhus* means typhus.

well as relapsing fever and enteric fever. Something has been said of syphilis in the Egyptian Expeditionary Force. In the Turkish Army it was endemic, and when the soldiers were fit seemed to affect them little, but now that they were suffering from exhaustion and malnutrition it ravaged them.

All these diseases were well known. One which was obscure in those days was pellagra, not infectious, the main cause of which appeared to be lack of protein. No British soldier developed it, but the Egyptians of the Labour Corps did on a big scale. It attacked the Turks still more fiercely and caused a great number of deaths among them.

But the biggest killers of all were malaria and influenza. The British medical officers had kept the incidence of malaria low by precautions such as oiling stagnant water, but were hopelessly handicapped in territory where no precautions had been taken, while the very malignant type of influenza was part of the "Spanish" disease which had swept over most of the whole world. The Turks, for obvious reasons, were far worse affected than the British by both. The total number of sick and wounded prisoners admitted into either Desert Mounted Corps field ambulances or Turkish hospitals in Damascus after the occupation—not counting those already there—was well over ten thousand.

Nor were these the only sufferers. Some ten thousand in a prisoners of war compound were also in a shocking state, and their numbers grew by thousands more transferred from another compound. They were placed under the care of Lieutenant-Colonel T. J. Todd, commanding the 10th Australian Light Horse. Todd had been badly wounded at Second Gaza and had never been fully restored to health. He was actually in hospital in Egypt when the offensive began, but this brought him out of his bed at once. An airman friend flew him to Jenin, where he rejoined his regiment and led it with his wonted ability. He took over a compound outside the city where the prisoners were a mob, without shelter even for the sick, and with no bandages, drugs, or disinfectants. The average daily death roll here was 170.

Colonel Todd squeezed what medical supplies he needed out of the Arab authorities in Damascus and requisitioned sheep for food. Realizing that reclamation had to be moral as well as physical, he formed the men into companies commanded by their own underofficers and set three Syrian doctors to work whom he had found among the prisoners. Finally, the daily death rate was brought down to fifteen. This heroic soldier later died at Luxor after the Mudros Armistice.[8]

The British battle casualties were small, and in the Desert Mounted Corps trifling. The situation was, however, reversed as regards disease. The infantry had indeed suffered very heavily from this cause and Chaytor's force still more, but neither was called on for further exertions and they were close to hospitals and railheads. The only division at a distance was the 7th Indian, now moving up the coast to Beirut. Practically all the rest of the troops returned to their former camps, which were free of the *Anopheles* mosquito. In the Desert Mounted Corps the malaria casualties leaped up sensationally, and taking the Egyptian Expeditionary Force as a whole, they doubled, rising to 5.51 per cent as against 2.85 in the month before the launching of the offensive. The 4th Cavalry Division had had all the bad luck that was going, since, after a very long spell in the Jordan Valley north of Jericho, it had returned to the river thirty-five miles higher up and spent several days at the extremely unhealthy Beisan.

The influenza scourge did not attack the British seriously until about October 6. Admissions from the Desert Mounted Corps amounted to 3,109 for the week ending on October 12, as against 1,246 for the preceding week. This was followed by a high proportion of cases of pneumonia. Unlike that of the Turks, the death rate was moderate, but in the course of October and November 479 British deaths occurred in the city, of which probably not twenty were due to wounds and an unknown number to other diseases. Devoted doctors and medical orderlies, often scarcely able to move from the effects of malaria and influenza, by their splendid service kept the figures down. Many patients had the good fortune to be carried by hospital ship to Egypt, but to get them aboard was a slow process owing to the state of the roads, railways, and ports.

So far the battle casualties of the Desert Mounted Corps were not much over five hundred: 125 killed, 362 wounded, and 43 missing, some of the last-named being found in Turkish hospitals in Damascus. Only 11 British officers and 5 Indian officers had been killed. And this was the price paid for a victory as overwhelming as Alexander the Great's over Darius at Arbela, where the Macedonians are variously said to have had one hundred, three hundred, and five hundred killed, with about a thousand horses, and the Persian figures are given with fantastic differences by three historians as 300,000, 90,000, and 40,000—it need hardly be said that the first estimate, that of Arrian, is moonshine. When the pursuit began, the British intelligence services estimated the number of Turks who had reached Damascus or had a prospect of reaching it to be 40,000, including of course officials and other noncombatants. Now the number of surviving Turks was reduced to half that figure and perhaps only a quarter of these were fit to fight. It seemed impossible that they could be made ready to fight at short notice, but though the only test to which they were to be subjected was slight, they actually were. This resistance was the feat of Mustapha Kemal, who had hitherto been eclipsed in this campaign by Jemal the Lesser. Apart from the fugitives, the only troops at his disposal were those of the skeleton Eighth Army quartered from a little north of Damascus to Bozanti in the Taurus. This army consisted of only four weak divisions—probably not above five thousand rifles in all, including some battalions of gendarmerie.

As in all cavalry actions and campaigns, the loss in horses was much higher than that of men, but still astonishingly low. Killed, died, or destroyed horses numbered only 1,021—under four per cent—with 259 missing. Even these figures must be excessive because the casualties were reported, not from September 19 but from week to week, and it is known that a good many horses were rejected and got rid of before the beginning of the offensive. Veterinary hospitals and mobile sections reported that between September 15 and October 5 they had taken in 3,245 horses out of a total of 25,618 in the force and had reissued as cured nearly a thousand of these. It was the seasoned horses that best withstood the strain. Recently acquired remounts seldom got as far as Damascus. The horsemastership had been superb. What must be realized is that the Yeomen and Australians rode on an average somewhere near 220 pounds, counting arms, ammunition, food, and heavy military saddles, and the Indians only about 15 pounds less. Barrow's Fourth Cavalry Division shone in this respect and far exceeded the record of the Fifth and the Australian Mounted Divisions. One company of the 19th Lancers, commanded by Captain G. M. Fitzgerald and composed of Sikhs, arrived at Damascus without the loss of a mount.

One of the most striking participants in these campaigns now quits the theater. Why did Lawrence go at the height of his fame and when there was so much valuable and fascinating work before him? It is impossible to penetrate his baffling mind, but it would seem that his first reason was atonement. He felt that the Arabs had been betrayed and that he had played a part in their betrayal. At the same time he felt disillusioned about them. He had never experienced the sentimentalism with which so many Britons regarded the "noble sons of the desert," but he had fallen under their spell. The spell was gone now, but it was replaced by determination to fight for their cause in Paris and London. Sheer physical exhaustion was undoubtedly another factor.[9] He made his own arrangements as regards this last. He already held the rank of temporary lieutenant-colonel; now he demanded and obtained that of temporary colonel because it brought with it the luxury of a sleeping berth on what was known as the Taranto route and three days for the trip instead of eight by a troop train. He afterwards spoke of this promotion as his "Taranto rank."[10] The route was by rail from Taranto, through Paris, to Cherbourg. He traveled with Chetwode, whom he greatly admired.

Soon after his arrival in London Lawrence was called to meet the Eastern Committee of the Cabinet. His proposals need not be discussed because they were not fulfilled, though the actual developments were not very different. A grave threat to the ambitions of the Arabs appeared when, in early November of 1918, M. Georges Picot arrived in Palestine with the title of "French High Commissioner in Syria and Armenia" and a week later reported to Paris that the country would continue to be as hostile to the French in Syria as it had been in Palestine. He advocated the despatch of a large force to Syria and a request to Britain to hand it over.

Next the French were perturbed by the news that the Emir Feisal was about to set out for London, traveling through France. The narrow-minded but well-meaning Colonel Brémond was by this time commanding his regiment at home and was ordered to meet the Emir, treating him as a person of distinction but according him no diplomatic status. Colonel Brémond set off, but was too late, meeting the Emir and Lawrence only at Lyons, Lawrence having already received Feisal on his landing from a British cruiser. Lawrence took the Emir in early December for a tour of England. When he accompanied Britain's guest to Buckingham Palace Lawrence wore Arab dress and received a reproof. King George V demanded whether he considered it fitting for a British officer to come into his presence wearing "foreign uniform."

In January 1919 Lawrence went to Paris to take part in the Peace Conference at Versailles. Accompanied by Feisal, he called on Colonel House, President Wilson's *alter ego*, with the proposal that the United States should step in and set up an American mandate in Syria.[11] This was an unwise and hopeless project, but in other respects he was to a considerable degree successful both in guiding Feisal—who, for all his ability and political experience in Turkey, which he had visited early in 1916, found himself out of his depth —and in pressing his cause. Lawrence would perhaps have

been more successful had he been able to conceal his hatred
of the French, which was patent to all.[12] He got on very well
with the British Prime Minister, Lloyd George, and deeply
impressed him by the lucidity with which he marshaled his
points.

Lawrence's return to Oxford in May was an unhappy
home-coming. His father had recently died and two of his
brothers had been killed in the war. Another visit to Paris
carried him no further. The French were adamant and the
British felt that they could do no more.

Lawrence played a great part in setting up Feisal in
Mesopotamia and Abdullah in what was then known as Trans-
Jordan, and if the Hashemite Kingdom has been bloodily
extinguished in Mesopotamia, Abdullah's grandson reigns in
Jordan and, if he survives, may be ranked as the greatest
figure of his house.

THE FINAL PHASE

10   THE FINAL STAGES of the campaign involved little fighting. They are, however, highly interesting by reason of the vast exertions they called forth from troops often near the end of their tether. These are part and parcel of the achievement of Allenby's cavalry, and of the last of its kind by horsed cavalry in the history of war. In the British Army today one section of the Royal Armoured Corps consists of the old cavalry regiments, who could have no better exemplars than their old selves, though only officers represented them in Palestine and Syria, a handful at that.

In a suburb of Damascus, Chauvel had established his headquarters in a house formerly occupied for a few days by the headquarters of Liman von Sanders. On October 3 Allenby came to see him and ordered him to capture Riyaq, the last military, as opposed to political, objective. It was 30 miles northwest of Damascus in the valley of the Nahr el Litani, or Dog River, in the gorge of which one conqueror after another has inscribed the record of his victories and conquests.

It is an impressive roll, of which only a few of the best-known captains can be mentioned. Look first at perhaps the greatest of the centuries before Christ and one of the few in those ages arousing sympathy in modern minds. Rameses

II represents Egypt at her greatest. A masterly soldier, his victories were won with a highly trained, disciplined, and equipped army, which was yet just short of the highest in spirit. It rolled forward with every precaution and struck deadly blows at the weakest points of its foes. Under his prudent leadership this perfect machine was virtually invincible, and victory and conquest alike were unstained by the bestialities of later invaders. After the subjugation of Palestine and Syria, Egypt showed that she knew how to rule. Her local governors were moderate, and officials of the conquered peoples were employed. She had a civilized attitude which made occupation relatively mild, but her decline and fall, when she became, as the Assyrians said, "a broken reed," made matters easier for these bloody invaders from the north.

The Assyrians were far more formidable fighters and especially when led by Ashur-nasir-pal. Their pictures which have come down to us exhibit an unmistakable wolfish type. Ahead rode a swarm of light cavalry, ravaging the country, destroying forces too weak to oppose them, spreading out to pass by those they found too formidable. They laid the foundations of victory, but the architects were their infantry bowmen, marching in close order. Woe to the vanquished! Ashur-nasir-pal flayed his prisoners or impaled them on stakes.

The next of his race is better known to readers of the Bible, and he was to get what he deserved. Hezekiah, the good King of Judah, was also a good fighter who had smitten the Philistines "even unto Gaza and the borders thereof," but after Sennacherib had routed Israel Hezekiah realized that he could not withstand the Assyrians. He therefore tried to buy Sennacherib off with the treasure of his palace and the House of the Lord, even cutting off the gold of the temple doors. The Assyrian took the spoil but then threatened to storm Jerusalem. Hezekiah's last hope lay in Jehovah, who did not fail him. Kings and Chronicles relate that "the Lord sent an angel which cut off all the mighty men of valour, and the leaders and captains of the King of Assyria," and Isaiah claims that he struck down "a hundred and fourscore and five thousand." We must suppose that some disease, more deadly even than those which afflicted Allenby's Turkish foes, swept through the ranks of the invaders. Sennacherib returned in shame, to be assassinated by his son.

Look forward to the sixteenth century A.D. Sultan Selim I of Turkey had a relatively easy task against indifferent opposition. It was made all the easier by the quarrels of the Christian kings, which had already permitted him to add northern Mesopotamia to the Ottoman empire. The Turks had very much the same reputation then as in the First World War. They entered Syria with no such broad sweep as had characterized the advance of the Assyrians because they had no such grasp on the handling of light forces. Brave, dour, stout in attack but more formidable still in defense, savage in war but with a certain standard of honesty in the keeping of engagements, in peace they were unexpectedly mild rulers of subject races so long as these gave no trouble. Yet this mildness was due, not to softness of heart, but to lethargy of mind. They wanted the least possible bother. There is nothing spectacular in the story of this invasion, which may be likened to the steady grinding of a vast mill. Having routed the Mamelukes at Aleppo, they pressed on to Egypt and secured it with little difficulty. It was still nominally a Turkish province at the outbreak of the First World War.

A British inscription was now shortly to be added to those on the tablets of the Dog River.

Riyaq was the junction between the standard-gauge railway from Constantinople and the narrow-gauge line to Palestine and the Hejaz. The Royal Air Force had bombed it severely the previous day, inflicting heavy damage to the little town and catching some of Kemal's forces, according to air reports several thousand, passing through.

Macandrew's 5th Cavalry Division set out on October 5, and was caught up by the 12th Light Armoured Motor Battery and the 7th Light Car Patrol before it had progressed far. Macandrew was in a hurry because he had been told that the Turks were clearing the station and depots, and he was prepared to sacrifice more horses to prevent them. However, the sacrifice was not required because subsequent reports indicated that the enemy had gone. He therefore canceled a night march which the 14th Brigade and the cars had been ordered to make, and these forces did not reach the place until 2 P.M. on October 6. A great deal of damage had been done, and many Turkish dead were found, but several locomotives and many tracks of both gauges, together with valuable stores, had survived.

It now seemed likely that the next stand made by Liman and Kemal would be in the mountainous region about Homs, which would afford many good defensive positions. However, the best defensive positions are of no worth if the defenders are inadequate, and the Turks were so disorganized that the commander-in-chief had abandoned all hope of offering any serious resistance this side of Aleppo, to which he had already sent Colonel von Oppen with the only reliable troops and on which the fresh divisions under Mustapha Kemal, with re-organized units in their ranks, were closing.

Meanwhile the Indian Division of the XXI Corps had marched up the coast road in three columns, starting on October 2. "Road" was at this time a complete misnomer for a section of the track known as "the Ladder of Tyre," and in fact Beirut had no communication with Acre and Haifa except by a circuitous way for mules and asses carrying goods in panniers and their riders on their rumps. When General Bulfin came forward to look at the Ladder, a mile of huge steps hewn out of the rock, he was told by the Chief Royal Engineer of the division, Lieutenant-Colonel E. F. J. Hill, that the blasting he was preparing might carry the whole shelf into the sea. Bulfin asked for "time for a couple of cigarettes" before reaching his decision. He chose to back his luck and with the happiest results. Not only this section but the whole cliff road was opened to wheeled transport within three days. The Queen's Own Royal Dragoons, or Glasgow Yeomanry, which was the corps cavalry regiment, was not held up and reached Tyre during the afternoon of October 4. At this point supplies for three days were brought in from the sea and picked up by each of the three columns as it arrived, and a further consignment was put ashore at Sidon. On October 8 the leading troops reached Beirut, to the cheers of the citizens, two-thirds of them Christians, as Beirut was the site of an American university which had given Syria its best scholars and scientists. French military governors were installed here and in the other two towns.

It was satisfactory from the point of view of the 5th Cavalry Division to have found the charred remains of thirty aircraft on Riyaq airfield, though these had been destroyed by the Turks themselves, not by British bombing. There was, however, to be further invaluable support from the air, particularly in the dropping of maps. The railway station and airfield at Aleppo were also bombed during this stage of the advance.[1]

The 5th Cavalry Division was now entering magnificent country, though spectacular scenery of this sort generally involves slow progress and long halts for the supplies to catch up. In this case the main road was reasonably good. The Turks had, unfortunately for the 5th Cavalry Division but to their own advantage, picked up the railway from Tripoli, forty miles north of Beirut, to Homs; and on the Beirut–Damascus line the rack-and-pinion system had been installed over twenty miles in the mountains of Lebanon, and lack of the specially-built engines prevented the movement of supplies straight through from Beirut to Damascus.[2] On the other hand, the country was far more fertile for grain crops—with the exception of oats, grown only a considerable distance farther north—and afforded better grazing for beasts than that which the Desert Mounted Corps had left behind. There was no lack of cattle, sheep, goats, wheat, and barley. Goats were invaluable because all the Indian troops ate them and the Hindoos held themselves profaned if the flesh of the sacred bullock touched their lips. The famous grapes on which the Republic of Lebanon now thrives hardly need mention. The vines were sometimes 5,000 feet up on the sides of hills.

On October 9 Allenby ordered the Desert Mounted Corps to advance on Homs and the XXI Corps to push the 7th Division forward to Tripoli. At the same time he accepted Feisal's proposal to employ a thousand cavalry and camelry to strike at the Turkish communications between Homs and Hama. Allenby ordered Chauvel and Bulfin to make all possible haste, and the head of Bulfin's column reached Tripoli on October 13, followed by the 19th Brigade under Brigadier-General W. S. Leslie.[3] Brigadier-General Weir had now taken over from Kelly in the command of the 13th Cavalry Brigade, and Leslie was his successor as C.O. of the 19th Infantry Brigade. Colonel de Piépape was appointed Military Governor of Beirut.

Macandrew's cars found the famous Baalbek clear of the enemy on October 10. By this time Chauvel was greatly worried by the appalling sick list of the 4th Cavalry Division. Left to himself he would have drawn it back to Damascus and substituted the Australian Mounted Division, but Allenby ruled that this would involve excessive delay and ordered him to advance at once. The Australians, in truth, were not in much better case. In a single week in October one of their brigades evacuated 61 per cent of its strength.[4] Macandrew moved in two columns, a day's march between them. There was now no need for great haste, and the 13th Brigade covered only 44 miles in three days, from October 13 to the 15th. Even before the start it had been reported that the Turks had abandoned Homs, which was reached on October 16. Once more the welcome was tumultuous. Macandrew was invited to an official banquet, at which, with his flair for saying the right thing, he spoke of the traditional friendship of the noble adversaries, Saladin and Richard Coeur de Lion. The division now enjoyed three days' rest.

Allenby, who had stayed several days with the 4th Cavalry Division, halted at Baalbek, had now finally decided to continue the advance to Aleppo. Just after the start of the campaign, the Chief of the Imperial General Staff, General Sir Henry Wilson, had in one of his flighty moods put for-

ward the project of a cavalry raid on the city. The commander-in-chief regarded this as a wildcat scheme which he
would not have touched with a poker.[5]*

If the War Cabinet were prepared to undertake a major
combined operation and land at Alexandretta Allenby would
play his part; otherwise he preferred to continue his operations
on the present lines. A landing in the Gulf of Iskenderun had
previously been discussed and had been very much in the mind
of Lord Kitchener. It had been first suggested to him by Sir
John Maxwell in December 1914 as "a vital blow at the railways" and to German interests. In October 1915 he had
strongly advocated it even before the evacuation of the Gallipoli Peninsula, but the objections of the Admiralty and War
Office had killed the suggestion.

Allenby ordered Chauvel to be ready for a continuance of
the 5th Division's advance by October 20, so that it could
reach Aleppo by the 26th. He also directed Bulfin to reinforce
him in cars. There was no difficulty in this, but the journey of
one unit merits attention. The 2nd Light Car Patrol was at
Sollum, more famous in a later war, still keeping an eye on the
Senussi. It moved on October 11 and went into action far
north of Hama on the 21st. It had covered roughly 1,200
miles, half by road, half by rail. To the present generation

* Wilson was a curious man to deal with. In 1917 he had proposed
to lend Allenby three or four divisions "for the winter." Allenby had
no reason to comment on this suggestion and did not do so, but he must
have regarded it as doubtful in the extreme, since the threat of reinforcement of the western front by German divisions from Russia was
already in the air and divisions were not always ready for transfer to
another theater at the moment they were needed. In July of that year
Wilson had established a special code known as "H. W. Personal," for
communication on particularly secret affairs with the commanders-in-
chief in all theaters. It may be said in passing that the system appears to
have been accepted by all of them, even Haig, except Allenby, who refused to use the method in "out" cables. The vicious result was that
the General Staff at the War Office was not allowed to take copies, that
the originals were destroyed by Allenby on receipt, and consequently
that they were not printed in the lists of secret telegrams published by
the War Office, though there were few better sources as regards strategy.
The present writer, when writing the official history of this campaign,
found only a few, and these of little account.

this may not seem remarkable, but in this phase of the development of the internal-combustion engine it was quite a feat. The 5th Division now had the strongest support yet: three light armored motor batteries and three light car patrols.

On October 20 came a crisis. Chauvel informed Allenby that the 5th Division was moving, but that the 4th Division, reduced to a fighting strength of 1,200, as against 2,500 in the already reduced 5th, was virtually incapable of marching, let alone fighting. Chauvel went on to say that Feisal would send 1,500 troops from Homs under Sherif Nasir, and hoped to call out many more Arabs as his march progressed. This expectation was fulfilled, Nasir being joined by a large force of the Anaze tribe.[6] The Arab contingent might prove valuable, but it could be little more than a gadfly to a reorganized Turkish army, of which some news had come through.

Allenby reacted by ordering the advance to cease and the 5th Cavalry Division to halt at Hama, 35 miles north of Homs, and Chauvel's message to this effect came to the hands of Macandrew on the evening of the 20th, after his first day's march. Macandrew's reply almost amounted to defiance. He had no difficulty in sending his comments immediately to Chauvel's advanced headquarters because the wires beside the railway were cut only here and there and the posts left standing. His message of October 20 ran: "Not understood. Troops far in advance and I propose advancing with armoured cars to Aleppo. Believe the railway road avoids all blown bridges. Shall be in Hama by midday tomorrow, which is already occupied. No opposition worth thinking of is expected at Aleppo. Hope advance may secure engines and rolling stock. Fivecav., 10:15 P.M." "Not understood" is rarely used by a commander to his superior because it is in effect a pejorative. It means, not so much that the message received is lacking in clarity—and there could be no mistaking the meaning here—as that it reveals a faulty intention. Next morning Chauvel sent the gist of the reply to the Chief of the General Staff at GHQ, Major-General Sir L. J. Bols.

Allenby did not hesitate. He loved a thruster and he

trusted Macandrew at his most headstrong. He ordered Bols to answer that he wanted to see Aleppo secured at the earliest possible moment. The episode redounds to the credit of both these vigorous cavalrymen.

Two days earlier the 5th Field Squadron Royal Engineers had begun to repair the big bridge over the Orontes north of Homs. The piers had not been destroyed, but had been seriously shaken when the central brick arch was blown out. Yet the work was finished at an early hour on October 21. That afternoon Macandrew entered Hama, a town of 10,000 inhabitants, with the 15th Brigade and the cars. On the next day the light car patrols were sent forward to establish touch with the Turks; but the first small rear guard did not await them, making off in trucks covered by a single armored car. The leading British cars pursued so fast that they caught up and took the Turkish armored car within a mile and pushed on after the trucks till the rearmost broke down. One of the historians of the campaign holds that the light car patrols and light armored batteries played a minor part, but evidence such as this refutes him. They could of course now take risks out of the question before the Turks had been broken up. When the cars bivouacked that night some 30 miles south of Aleppo they had left the leading column of the cavalry two days' march in the rear. However, it was speedily made clear that the Turkish reorganization was going on apace and that Mustapha Kemal was not to be bluffed. Going forward again, they discovered a force, the strength of which they could not ascertain because it was entrenched but which they put down at between two and three thousand, three miles south of Aleppo. By Macandrew's orders Captain R. H. M. McIntyre, commanding the 7th Light Car Patrol, went forward under a flag of truce to demand the surrender of the city. The written reply from Kemal's chief of staff was brief and to the point: "The Commander of the Turkish Garrison of Aleppo does not find it necessary to reply to your note."

The 15th Brigade joined the car column a short way south of Aleppo. As soon as the brigade attacked from the south, said Colonel Nuri Bey, his Arabs would co-operate from the east. In point of fact this energetic man beat his British allies to the goal and actually took over their front. On the afternoon of October 25 he attacked from the south, but was beaten back. Then he launched an assault from the east and broke in. Liman describes this as the first hard fighting since his troops had left Palestine. Liman was at Adana, over 100 miles from the scene, but he describes accurately what followed and gives the strength of the Bedouin at about fifteen hundred, which is correct. The Arabs took the citadel, but were driven out and abandoned the city. The fighting could do no harm to the citadel, built by Saladin's son; since this magnificent work, one of the most splendid of its kind in the world, had been allowed by the Turks to crumble to a shell. The German commander-in-chief goes astray at this time about the British. He states that they brought up a strong force of infantry in trucks, whereas what the Turks actually saw was a supply column and the maintenance vehicles of the cars.[7] Kemal withdrew from Aleppo with his force intact and established a fresh position north of the city.

The 15th Brigade still consisted of only two regiments, Jodhpore and Mysore Lancers, since the Hyderabad Lancers were still on the lines of communication. It was without artillery support, not that this mattered, since even a horse artillery battery could not have marched with it by the route it took. As he moved forward, Brigadier-General Harbord's sole information was an air report that some three hundred cavalry had been seen on the main road running northwest towards Alexandretta 8 miles away. Shortly afterwards, however, another message came in that about a thousand Turks with two guns had quitted Aleppo that morning. Two squadrons of the Jodhpores then trotted forward and, as they topped a slight ridge, came in sight of the village of Haritan and at the same moment came under machine-gun fire. They fell back a quarter of a mile, dismounted, and took up a position straddling the road.

There was no reconnaissance, and the only information

Harbord had received about the enemy, apart from the cavalry, was that a rather smaller party of infantry was in position just south of Haritan. He ordered the Mysores to move round the ridge and charge and the remaining squadrons of the Jodhpores to follow them. He got no support from the light cars; the 12th Light Armoured Battery, moving over higher ground, was so hotly engaged by the Turkish machine guns that it drew back after a number of tires had burst. The Senior Special Service Officer with the Mysore Lancers, Major W. J. Lambert, now sighted the Turkish left, considerably farther east than had been suspected, and ordered the regiment to charge. It dashed forward with the three leading squadrons in line of squadrons. The Turks at this particular point were fortunately only 150 strong, and the Mysores swept through them, spearing 50 and taking 20 prisoners.

Meanwhile Lieutenant-Colonel Holden, the Senior Special Service Officer with the Jodhpores, who had so distinguished himself at Haifa early in the offensive, had halted his two leading squadrons in dead ground and sent a mounted messenger for news. Major Lambert sent the man back with the message that he was about to attack once more and a request that the Jodhpores should advance and cover his regiment while it rallied for the charge. They immediately did so, and the Mysores, slightly shaken by their experience, re-formed about a thousand yards behind. However, Holden came at once under even heavier fire; he himself was at once killed; and the two leading squadrons retired in confusion. Captain H. P. Hornsby rallied one and turned to charge, the second following. Almost at once he was shot down. A good Indian squadron commander, observing the strength of the enemy and that reinforcements were coming up, wheeled and fell back, leaving the Special Service Officer apparently dead. Actually Hornsby, with a bullet through his neck, recovered consciousness and was able to creep to safety on all fours after the fall of night.[8] It looked as though the Turks, now seen to be about three thousand strong, were preparing a counterattack, but this did not follow. The position of the reduced 15th Brigade was nevertheless perilous until the 14th Brigade arrived on the scene late that night. At midnight it was reported that the Turks had withdrawn.

So the last action of a campaign in which the enemy had hitherto been beaten at every point ended with a success for him, slight though it was. For the enemy, one man, and one alone, had gained it. The first reason why the Turks had fought as stoutly as they did and had shaken off their demoralization is to be found in the personality and organizing power of the future Ghazi, Mustapha Kemal Pasha. The majority of his force had gone through the disastrous battles and retreats, but they had recovered a good part of their traditional quality after being rested, re-equipped, and inspired afresh. Kemal had the advantage that he had been able to feed them better than they had ever been fed since Murray invaded Palestine; in those bad days, a corps commander said later, the only time he had had a really good meal was when a German princeling had come on a visit and had brought his own nosebag. Kemal did not lead his army from behind. An officer of Arab blood who passed after the war into the service of the Emir Abdullah in Trans-Jordan, informed the writer of the official history that he fought a machine gun in the affair at Haritan and that the fire was controlled and directed by Kemal in person.[9]

The British had themselves to blame in one respect. There was no ground reconnaissance, though there was time and opportunity for it. They relied entirely on the air reports. However, this was put into the shade by the fine performance of two Imperial Service Regiments, the troops of the independent princes, which before the war had been regarded as a doubtful asset, though they had, of course, been thoroughly trained since. The losses had been small in the circumstances, 80 men, with a doubtless considerably greater, though unrecorded, number of horses—few indeed in view of the disparity of numbers.

By October 30 the Turks held a position at least 25 miles in length bestriding the sharply bending road to Alexandretta

at two points 12 miles NNW. of Haritan, with outposts 4
miles in advance. They had four divisions, totaling perhaps
eight thousand rifles, including one regiment brought up from
Constantinople. In the Taurus or on the coast were three or
four weak divisions. The Turkish cavalry division and nine
infantry divisions had been disbanded or destroyed. The
British had captured 75,000 prisoners, about 3,700 being Germans and Austrians, 360 guns, and 89 locomotives. On all
fronts Turkey had lost 325,000 killed, 240,000 from disease,
and it is estimated over a million, temporarily or permanently,
by desertion.[10] The wounded cannot be counted.

British losses were light, very light by comparison with
those of Allenby's first offensive up to the taking of Jerusalem. From September 19 to October 31 there were 71 officers killed, 249 wounded, 3 missing; 782 rank and file killed,
4,179 wounded, 382 missing—a total of 5,666. Of these the
Desert Mounted Corps lost only 650. From the attack on the
Suez Canal in January 1915 to October 31, 1918, the losses
were 51,451, but casualities from malaria, dysentery, diarrhea,
venereal disease, and a few others, totaled 503,377, with a
small proportion of deaths.[11]

Meanwhile the Allied armies in Macedonia under the
supreme command of the French General Franchet d'Espèrey
had won an overwhelming victory. It was so complete that
the Turkish grand vizier had informed the British naval commander-in-chief in the Mediterranean, Vice-Admiral the Hon.
Sir S. A. Gough-Calthorpe, that the Sultan was prepared to
conclude a separate peace. The affair was a somewhat painful
drama, since it marked a bitter conflict between Britain and
France, and the former's success was to rankle for a long
time. Franchet d'Espèrey had not invited any British representative to take part in negotiating—or, rather, dictating—
the Bulgarian armistice; now Britain was determined that the
French should have no part in the Turkish. After long and
difficult discussions, in which the British admiral showed remarkable coolness and even sympathy for the defeated, the

armistice was signed in the battleship *Agamemnon* late on October 30, on the British side by the admiral alone. On the same day Marshal Liman von Sanders received a cable from the grand vizier ordering him to hand over his command and return to Constantinople. This came as no surprise, and he was able to set out next day. Liman asserts that it was owing to the exertions of the grand vizier—not one of the three Turkish signatories—that the German contingent in Syria was given free passage home. These troops were prepared for what was coming and entrained as quickly as possible. Liman himself had an unhappy experience. Arriving at Malta on February 3, 1919, he was there detained until August 21. Typically, he takes the dignified course in his book of mentioning the facts and withholding comment. The British had to consider a number of charges of war crimes. A long examination of these proved that he had, on the contrary, striven to alleviate the lot of prisoners of war and restrain Turkish cruelties.[12]

The armistice contained 25 clauses, but only the most important facts need be given here:

(*1*) Opening of the Dardanelles and Bosporus and Allied occupation of their forts.

(*4*) Allied prisoners of war and Armenians to be handed over to the Allies.

(*5*) Demobilization of the Turkish army, except for troops watching the frontiers and preserving internal order.

(*6*) Surrender of warships in Turkish and Turkish-occupied waters.

(*7*) The Allies to have the right to occupy any strategic point in case of a threat to their security.

(*10*) Allied occupation of the Taurus tunnel system.

(*13*) Prohibition to destroy any naval, military or commercial material.

(*16*) Surrender of the garrisons in the Hejaz, Assir, Yemen, Syria, and Mesopotamia.

(*19*) All Germans and Austrians to be evacuated within one month.

(22) Turkish prisoners to be kept at the disposal of the Allied Powers.

(23) Obligation on the part of Turkey to end relations with the Central Powers.

(25) Hostilities between the Allies and Turkey to cease at noon, local time, on October 31, 1918.

Turkey's appalling situation had been brought about more by the Bulgarian rout in Macedonia than by her own downfall in Syria. After the Allied victory, the commander-in-chief in Macedonia decided to advance to the Danube with the intention of knocking Austria-Hungary out of the war. He requested the British commander, General G. F. Milne, to take command of the right, with three of his four divisions remaining in the theater. Milne considered Constantinople as important a goal as the Danube, but, though perturbed by the fact that the Frenchman evidently regarded Constantinople as secondary, did not raise any abrupt objections. He did, however, later recommend to the chief of the Imperial General Staff that the troops of a single nationality should be employed against the Turks, that they should be British, with a British admiral for combined operations and the protection of supplies, and that British troops should not go north. Milne's first reason was British tradition. As his chief of the general staff, Major-General G. N. Cory, put it to the writer of the official history of the Macedonian campaign: "Never, if you have an alternative, go where the Navy cannot hold out a hand to you."

The second argument was still more cogent. It was probably first enunciated by the First Sea Lord, Vice-Admiral Sir Rosslyn Wemyss, who said that the Allied fleet, under a British commander-in-chief, should by the terms of an armistice with Turkey, pass through the Dardanelles and Bosporus into the Black Sea, as "a proper recognition" of the fact that Britain had had the lion's share in hostilities against Turkey. The Prime Minister, Lloyd George, held the same opinion. After much debate two divisions were recalled and the third did not go very far.

Franchet d'Espèrey's operation was a triumph. He reached the Danube, wrung an armistice from revolutionary Hungary, but was forestalled in his intention to do the same with Austria by the Allies in Italy and not permitted to march on Dresden.

On his side, General Milne's march was bloodless. The Turks made no resistance; the armistice was signed; the Allied fleets, led by Gough-Calthorpe in the *Téméraire*, steamed through; Constantinople was occupied.

Milne had a tough job enough in dealing with the Turks, but Allenby's was probably tougher to start with. The least of his worries was that General Fakri Pasha, commanding the garrison of Medina, refused to surrender. Finally, in January 1919, his officers laid hands upon him in a sickbed and delivered him to the Arabs. The prisoners sent to Egypt numbered 7,636 officers and men, and a good many Arabs and Syrians volunteered for service under Hussein in the Hejaz. Allenby had to face continual obstruction, bland in words, stubborn in deeds, and make a good hand of his dreary task.

It took longer to make peace with Turkey than to defeat her in war. The war lasted four years to a day, from October 30, 1914, when the British Ambassador had demanded his passport. Peace with Turkey under the Treaty of Lausanne— substituted for the abortive Treaty of Sèvres—required four years and nine months. The new Turkey, shorn of her Arab lands, and from her point of view well rid of them, was to be the creation of Mustapha Kemal, the Ghazi.

Once Allenby's famous temper took control. One night a thief from the village of Surafend, notorious nest of thieves, pulled from under a New Zealand trooper's head a bag which served him as a pillow. The man sprang up in pursuit, but was shot dead with a revolver. His comrades surrounded the village. Without waiting for GHQ's examination of the evidence, they then after several days entered it, passed out the women and children, and set about killing the males. How many were killed is unknown, but the butcher's bill was high and scarcely a man in the village was left unmaimed. To make assurance doubly sure, the New Zealanders burned the Bedouin encampment close by—still, as from the first, watched and applauded by the Australians. Allenby naturally called for the names of the leaders in the killing, but equally naturally got no response. He then had the brigades formed in hollow square, and, though his indignation was praiseworthy, his language was far from being so. The New Zealanders and the whole division would have accepted punishment, which they knew they deserved, but they did not accept his abuse. The bitterness went on into the middle of 1919, when an Australian went to visit Allenby in Cairo and reported how unhappy the situation was. Could he not do something to mend it? No. Allenby never apologized and here he would not take back a word. What he did was to issue a loving farewell order to the Anzacs who remained, the first embarkations having taken place early in 1919.

"I knew the New South Wales Lancers and the Australian Horse well in the Boer War," he began, going on to praise the fighting qualities of all the men from the antipodes. They had, he said, proved themselves equally good afoot, on the defensive or showing in dismounted action the dash and enterprise of the best light infantry. He made a good point in talking of their "restless activity of mind".[13]

Both sides had been in the wrong, but the troops more than the commander-in-chief, whereas the Australian official history gives the impression that they had been equally so.* The offence of the New Zealanders was heinous and called for anger, particularly so, because, though attrocities have been a commonplace of many wars, none had been exhibited in Palestine. As for the commander-in-chief's reaction, it was certainly sharp but not unique. Nor is the soldier often upset by anger. "Quiet nagging and sarcasm," this writer remarked in a booklet published during the Second World War, "do more to sour the soldier than explosions of temper, to which martial men in the high ranks have always been subject, and to which

* This volume was written by H. S. Gullett, who had come out originally as a trooper in the Light Horse. The excellent practice of compiling notes throughout a campaign, introduced on a big scale by the Americans in the Second World War, was rare in the First.

those in the lower are well enough accustomed." What about Condé, Napoleon, Wellington, Montgomery, and Patton?

Most of the Light Horse had to play their part in the suppression of the Egyptian nationalist rising of 1919. However, two regiments embarked in March and before the summer all but a few men employed at bases were on their way home. The British divisions were less fortunate in that for them duties of occupation lasted longer, but individual men were shifted rapidly under the system of demobilization. They came home carrying their heads high, and survivors still do. They are clannish and like to meet. One first-class London Territorial battalion still musters about seventy-five of all ranks for its annual dinner, and one of the company is the sergeant to whom the civic authorities offered in vain the keys of Jerusalem.

LESSONS OF THE CONFLICT

11 THE FIRST LESSON of the campaign is the old one, that there is a wide gulf between merely skilled and inspired leadership. This may sound a platitude, but before examining Armageddon let us look back for a moment to earlier days. When the then Lieutenant-General J. C. Smuts arrived in the country in early February 1918, Allenby had captured Jerusalem and Jaffa, but with very high losses as compared with those of his final offensive. The Supreme War Council had recently decided that Turkey was the weakest link in the hostile coalition and that the Entente forces should therefore stand on the defensive from the opening of the year in France, Italy, and the Balkans and "undertake a decisive offensive against Turkey with a view to the annihilation of the Turkish forces and the collapse of Turkish resistance."

The British Prime Minister, Lloyd George, believed passionately in this strategy and had indeed inspired, so far as he could, the Joint Note of the Military Representatives at Versailles which embodied it. General Sir W. Robertson had been hostile. When a relatively junior officer, Wavell, still liaison officer between the War Office and the Egyptian Expeditionary Force, was asked for his views, he found the

Military Representatives at Versailles unduly optimistic and the chances of a victory such as they looked forward to distinctly less good than they believed. Wavell was surprised that there was no conception of the difficulties facing an advance to Damascus and Aleppo. He wrote: "As far as can be judged from the morale and attitude of the Turks in Palestine, there seems no good reason to believe that another defeat or even the occupation of Damascus and Aleppo would cause them to rise against their German masters and conclude a separate peace."[1] Nothing that occurred in the Armageddon campaign belied this forecast. Where grand strategy is concerned, the defeat of Germany on the western front proved to the Turks that the war was lost. The immediate reason why they threw up their hands was, however, the rout of Bulgaria and the opening of the road to Constantinople.

At the time of the Military Representatives' Note and Wavell's commentary on it the *sine qua non* was a crushing victory, in which speed would be a major factor. How did Smuts plan for victory? First of all let us recognize that he was one of the most brilliant minds of modern times and a much cleverer man than Allenby. As a very young man in the Second Boer War he had proved himself a first-class soldier, as the British wryly remembered. In this First World War he had proved successful in East Africa, though his conduct of the campaign had been subject to some criticism, and he had been extremely optimistic in his belief that it was as good as over when he gave up the command. His advice began well: an advance to the Jordan and thence the demolition of the Hejaz Railway to isolate Turkish troops from Ma'an to Medina. The rest of his advice was of very different quality: The standard-gauge railway would be pushed forward to Haifa, thence probably to Beirut. The advance of the main body of the Egyptian Expeditionary Force would take place with it and at the same pace. A secondary column would march with the railway across the Plain of Esdraelon, from Haifa through Dera on Damascus in conjunction with the Arabs and Druses. Another 388 miles of rails would be needed for a double track to Haifa and a single to Beirut. Among the extra labor required he suggested two Canadian railway battalions.

This was how Murray had advanced across Sinai but shorn of all the arguments that Murray could muster to support his policy; it was throwing away practically every advantage that Allenby possessed: preponderance of strength, large in infantry and artillery, immense in cavalry; command of the sea, so nearly absolute where operations were concerned that there was virtually no danger from submarines involved in landing supplies even at ports which were mere open roadsteads; transport of far better quality than that of his foe and much larger, even in proportion to his strength; much greater weight in heavy artillery to aid the speediest breakthrough and therefore insure surprise.

History has many lessons to teach us that a plan which seeks security at the expense of surprise and mobility is the depth of unsoundness.[2] We may say with confidence that, but for the spring victories of the Germans in France and the consequent stripping of the Egyptian Expeditionary Force, Allenby would have defeated the Turks heavily, but it is very doubtful whether he would have reached Damascus. He would have inflicted a far heavier blow if he had followed his own first plan, but, again, it would not have been hard enough. A man of Allenby's type, the last one would normally describe as brilliant, will often enough produce something better than the first-class intellectual, not only in war but in the law courts, in the directors' room, and at the operating table.

So the situation called for speed involving the acceptance of risks. This was so from the first moment, but within a very short space of time the call became more insistent. Now it was above all a dozen diseases that demanded speed and boldness.[3] If the cavalry did not get quickly to Damascus and Aleppo it would never get there at all. Allenby took the risks. At the same time, however, he showed his qualities of leadership by halting Major-General Sir George Barrow's 4th Cavalry Division when the division became prostrated by influenza and malaria, and by yielding to Major-General Macandrew's plea that he should be permitted to go on to Hama and thence to Aleppo at a moment when Allenby himself had decided that a single division was inadequate for the task and would be in peril of defeat should the Turks prove sufficiently reorganized and sufficiently bold to attack.

Next we come to the moral element. On the western front the influence of the commander-in-chief and of his army leaders had to be exercised upon the troops in the main through their subordinates. Over the heads of all in 1918 stood Foch, who in the early days of the war had proved himself a great inspirer of men and, as a corps and army commander, had lived up to his precept that the leader of forces must produce the driving force. Foch found himself obliged to abandon any close, even momentary, contact with the troops themselves, and exercised his will through his generals. The commander-in-chief who was most successful in inspiring a vast force was probably Franchet d'Espèrey, who had done so in France up to the height of an army group command and did it again to a great extent in Macedonia as commander-in-chief, though he had twenty-six infantry divisions as against Allenby's seven and they were of five nationalities: French, British, Greek, Serbian, and Italian.

The strength of the Egyptian Expeditionary Force was above that which most of the best army commanders could have tackled in this way. Allenby did it superbly, and his triumph was due in considerable measure to his physical strength and endurance. Mention has been made of the trust and admiration he won from his Australian troops, though he was a strict disciplinarian—Gullett calls him a severe one. One habit of his when visiting the Jordan sector was to fly into a rage at sight of the mounted troops riding in shorts. It sounds tyrannical, but his fits of temper actually had a sound basis. Hot men on hot horses were prone to blood poisoning and dangerous sores because their bare knees rubbed against the horses' flanks. The Australian official historian records that on one occasion during a reconnaissance, "an Australian leader on the flank, who after two hours' vexatious delay had succeeded in getting in touch by heliograph with his brigade and was sending an urgent operation message, was held up while he received a heliograph that the Commander-in-Chief was in the Valley, and that any officer whose men were found in shorts would be severely dealt with."[4]

As a result the men, who had no change of clothing in the Valley, were condemned to wear riding breeches and leggings. Finally, however, Allenby compromised, after much discussion, by permitting them to ride in khaki drill slacks. The Australians had been much annoyed but, though they cursed him in their inimitable fashion, their sense of humor, combined with their belief in him, prevented the spread of bitterness. Surely it was an admirable compromise, even though held up too long. Anyhow, the Australians and other troops had their grapevine. When Allenby was coming on a visit a code message was sent out, the interpretation of which was "Bull broken loose."

"The only period of the whole campaign which has the interest created by the clash of two great strategists is that from November 6, 1917—which may be taken as the date on which Marshal von Falkenhayn assumed effective control of the Turkish armies in the field—to the end of the year. Throughout these disastrous weeks Falkenhayn never lost grip of the situation and never despaired. His two counter-offensives—that launched on November 12 against the British right flank during the advance up the coast, and still more the assault upon their communications in the hills between November 27 and December 1—were excellently contrived. In each case Falkenhayn effected a notable concentration, considering the slenderness of his means, and struck as hard as he could. The first blow was parried by mobility—the Australian Mounted Division, wide of the right flank, being able to yield ground without endangering the main body. . . . In the case of the second blow, the British had no such recourse. Every yard of ground was valuable here, and the attack had to be gradually worn down by stubborn defense. Falkenhayn's last great operation, the attempt to recapture Jerusalem at the end of December, was less well advised . . . He asked of his men more than they could give . . . and it was only by bitter experience that he learnt."[5]

The great difference between the strategy in the final phase and in the offensive of September 1917 is that in the former Allenby committed the cavalry to no fighting to breach the Turkish front, so that it could, relatively fresh and without having suffered loss, await the moment when the infantry swung open the gate for it.

As pointed out again and again, the most interesting feature of the campaign after Allenby's arrival and the later reorganization of the cavalry was the success of shock action. Almost every charge was made in extended formation and driven home at a genuine gallop, less frequent in war than military annals often suggest. On many occasions it was not the speed of the charge alone but the celerity with which brigadiers and regimental commanders made up their minds which led to success. When the Turkish troops encountered were already demoralized, charges succeeded without much cover from fire and none from artillery, but to undertake one without full reconnaissance by officers, the more senior the better, was to incur heavy risks. The cavalry brigade had normally a horse-artillery battery attached; it had its machine-gun squadron and the regimental Hotchkiss troops. However great the enemy's demoralization, the moral factor was unlikely to become preponderant during a mounted approach, and it was during this phase that covering fire was all important. If one action rather than another be selected as outstanding, it is the capture of Haifa and Mount Carmel. On the other hand, there is really only one sharp repulse to be recorded, that of Irbid. It must be added that when a charge was delivered, the Turks always seemed to be more scared by the lance, when troops equipped with it were present, than by the sword.

The cavalryman's best friend, his horse, played its part nobly. Its endurance in the last offensive was extraordinary, but we must recognize that the calls made upon it on this occasion were lighter than those in the autumn of 1917 because grain, fodder, and water were more plentiful. On the other hand, some of the marches were longer; though after the Third Battle of Gaza the Lincolnshire Yeomanry—one of the many Yeomanry regiments sent to France and disbanded in the spring of 1919—went three days and nights without water, doing continuous work all the while. It is not always possible, from the British official volume, *Veterinary Services*, to identify the record of the horses as belonging to any particular period. This well-written account, however, is worth quoting for other instances of endurance and, it may be added, of horsemastership. The Australians' and New Zealanders' records are not available except for the two divisions as a whole.

The cavalrymen had absorbed the lesson that grooming—which is for the horse what massage is for the man, except that the one needs it always and the other only in emergency or in athletic training—was vital. "As the campaign continued, the average light horseman spent far more than the regulation time in rubbing down his coveted waler, and tired men would walk miles if there was a chance of acquiring a bundle of green fodder or an extra nosebag of grain."[6]

Certain units of the 4th Cavalry Division, in the case of Yeomanry again in 1917, are of interest as examples. The Bucks Yeomanry's longest period without water was 72 hours; during this period it was continually at work, and the average amount of grain and fodder issued daily was 10 lbs. to November 26 ... forage was obtained locally once only. The Dorset Yeomanry went 54 hours without water on one occasion, during which it covered sixty miles. The horses' average daily food was 9 lbs. of grain with 7 lbs. tibben (chopped straw) occasionally. Both were once obtained locally. The horses of the 20th Brigade R.H.A. had a harder task, with guns and ammunition to drag. Its record was 56 hours without water, in which it marched 50 miles, with an issue of 9 lbs. of grain; but its requisitioning of grain on three occasions is described as "considerable." These figures are abstracts from *Veterinary Services*, Chapter XI, which is worth study. Virtually out of date from the military point of view, it is not so for horse-lovers and long-distance riders.

We may leave aside the donkeys, useful as they were, because they were employed nearly always with the infantry in the hill country. The camels, however, merit a few words. They numbered in round figures thirty thousand, and though they required to fill their substantial stomachs seldom, they needed great quantities of water when they did so. They were least satisfactory off the roads in the Judaean hills or over Jordan, especially when the ground was slippery after rain, but even in such conditions gave invaluable service. It was difficult to train Britons and Australians to work with them, but it could be done, and even here the occasional expert turned up unexpectedly. On one occasion in a training camp an officer asked if there was anyone with experience of the beasts. One hand was held up, and on being asked what the experience amounted to, the soldier answered that it was in a large circus at home. The hour had found its man. Although the brigade of the Imperial Camel Corps, a fighting unit with fast beasts of a riding type, had long ago been broken up and the camels employed in transport were replaced as far as possible by mechanized or horse-drawn vehicles and were cut down drastically as uneconomic in the circumstances of the final offensive, camels were used in large numbers right up to the end.

Allenby was sparing of speech and still more of writing, and when he wrote letters they were more often concerned with birds and flowers than with his campaigns. He had, however, to send in dispatches to the Secretary of State for War of a type which must be peculiar to the British Army. There is no reason to suppose that he himself penned a line of the dispatch dated June 28, 1919—virtually no commander-in-chief wrote one, the exception being General Sir Ian Hamilton, whose dispatch on Gallipoli is marked all through by his vivid and attractive literary style. One may be sure, however, that Allenby inspired the general content and the particular points which he considered to be important. The most striking passage is marked by a frankness which exhibits a pleasing and unusual modesty.

"The course of the campaigns in this theatre followed closely the course of events in the main Western theatre.

"Thus, the first period, the defence of the Canal, corresponded to the first check of the enemy's onrush in France and Belgium; the period of the advance through the Sinai desert, to the general development of the Allied strength and the building up of a secure battle line along the whole front; the 1917 advance to the period of increased Allied pressure which exhausted the enemy's reserves; while the last advance coincided with the final Allied counteroffensive."[7]

Here, then, is a commander who gained a brilliant and memorable success in the Eastern theater of the war announcing that all its moves, the successes and checks suffered by his predecessor Murray and himself, had been governed by the fortunes of the western front. It may be argued that Allenby took the view prevalent on the western front because he had served there nearly three years and in Palestine and Syria for a year and a quarter, so that the former may be regarded as his spiritual home. This, however, would be an absurdity in view of his obvious happiness in exercising supreme command in a theater of rapid movement and extreme interest. At the same time we must beware of the fallacy prevalent among "Easterners" that, because Allenby now had a chance to exhibit his particular virtues, he may be ranked as second-rate on the western front and first-rate in this new theater of war. If there were any truth in this it would be true also of Stanley Maude, who had likewise served in France and also on the Gallipoli Peninsula before becoming commander-in-chief in Mesopotamia, and who reversed a record of defeat and shame which had no parallel in Palestine at its unhappiest moment to become the British public's "favourite son" before he died of cholera in Baghdad.

The "Easterner," who in his extreme type is nearly always a civilian, can fairly advance the claim that the finest prospect of the war was lost in the Gallipoli campaign, that even if the Turks had continued the war after the surrender of Constantinople their effort would soon have been brought to an end by the combined forces of the western Allies and Russia. He can fairly assert that the priority—especially in ammunition, in which for a time the western front was starved—given to Gallipoli by the Coalition Government formed in May 1915 was sound strategy. He is justified in his belief that a magnificent chance was thrown away by grave mismanagement and that if it had been seized the aid given to Russia in her distress would have been immensely greater.

"If the Dardanelles had been opened, so would the Bosporus, and the vast merchant fleets immobilized within would have been set free. Russia would not have suffered such a defeat as she did at German hands. But to go on to declare that Russia would have been saved from revolution and the world from communism is speculation."[8]

After the failure of the Gallipoli compaign there was no theater which could equal it in potential value. Henceforth, wherever French or British forces were sent in Europe they would find German reinforcements awaiting their arrival because the admirably managed German railways, never laid before the war without an eye on strategy, could beat troopships out of sight for speed—four and a half days to send four corps of eight divisions from France to Russia or in the reverse direction. Even including Italy, which had fairly good rail communications with France, the combined German and Austrian railways had a far higher capacity. In the more distant theaters of Mesopotamia and Palestine, there were either no combatant Germans but airmen, as in Mesopotamia, or relatively small contingents, as in Palestine, that had to be reckoned with, but Allied victory in neither of these greatly affected the Central Powers. The second-best opportunity after Gallipoli was probably that of the international army group in Macedonia, which drove first Bulgaria, then Turkey, out of the war, though very late in the day. The third best was in Palestine and Syria. Last come Mesopotamia; for all its triumphant close, it was allotted a disproportionate strength from Britain's war potential.

The defense of Egypt and the Suez Canal, like that of the Mesopotamia oilfields, was of course a necessity. How could it have been most economically assured? Possibly by holding the line of El 'Arîsh-Kossaima, between eight and thirty miles from the Palestinian frontier, as Murray had decided to do before he undertook his luckless invasion. The defense of the western front against the German spring offensives on the Somme and Lys was dangerously weakened by the strength left in Allenby's hands until the last moment, though from the administrative point of view the speed with which he was stripped of troops was highly creditable and effective.

The army with which Allenby achieved his magnificent final success was, however, not open to this objection. It contained only a single all-British infantry division, the 54th, which had remained as a reserve for the western front and had been at one moment under orders to go there. The rest of the infantry was composed in the main of relatively raw Indian battalions, unsuited to that theater. The excellent Indian regiments which made up the bulk of the 4th and 5th Cavalry Divisions could be spared, and there was no Australian or New Zealand infantry in the theater. If, therefore, we start with the offensive of September 1918 we can say confidently that it was fully justified.

It must be added that the Turkish command realized the importance of the Western theater. The news of the German victory in March came to it as a stimulus. It was not until mid-August that the Turkish commanders had the slightest doubt of success so complete that their allies must end the war within a matter of weeks; and probably not until well into September that they began to despair. This confidence was actually of value to the British, because it tended to induce the enemy to neglect the Palestine front, so that when fortune ceased to smile upon Germany the Turks suffered disastrous defeat. We therefore conclude that the "Easterner" has matters all his own way as regards Allenby's second offensive. Here he has an irrefutable argument, but the base on which it is constructed is far from being wholly sound.

WHAT GOOD CAME OF IT
AT LAST?

12 How is old Kaspar, his work done, to answer little Wilhemine and young Peterkin? The good and the bad that came out of Armageddon are more complex than the aftermath of Blenheim. In attempting a summary we should confine ourselves to the results of Allenby's final campaign.

First come the three major pledges: to the Arabs, to the Jews, and to the French. There is no need to return to the moral side, since this has already been sufficiently discussed; all that can be emphasized is that the promises could not be reconciled in full. Palestine was one of the colonial territories which were to be held by "Mandate" under the League of Nations. The immediate difficulty was French ambition. By force of arms Feisal was expelled from Damascus by General Gouraud in July 1920. After much bargaining, during which he visited England to plead for support, Feisal was compensated by the throne of Iraq, as the "Mesopotamia" of the war was now named. This was the work of Winston Churchill, at whose elbow stood Colonel T. E. Lawrence. Feisal's brother Abdullah received the Emirate of Trans-Jordan, later elevated to the status of Kingdom of the Jordan. Their father, King Hussein, had no such good fortune. His hostility to Ibn Saud, the man of the future in Arabia, was too great and the ferocity of the latter's Wahabis, the Puritans of the Muslim world, too overwhelming for his survival. He was driven from Mecca, to die an exile, and the Hejaz was added to the conqueror's dominions. The British Government had done its utmost to discharge its debt of honor to Feisal and Abdullah, but not to the Arabs in Palestine. The Jews, the greater part of them from Central Europe, were surging into the country, the influx, starting soon after the war, trebling within the first twelve to fifteen years and swelling to sevenfold not long afterwards. While Field-Marshal Lord Plumer remained in the country, governing, as it was said, by his bushy eyebrows, all was quiet, though he had no troops whatever; but immediately his formidable figure departed his successor had to face an Arab revolt which was not extinguished without bloodshed. And the bitterness created by this conflict was not confined to Palestine and Syria, or to the Arab peoples, but spread to all Muslims, notably those of India.

These few notes have taken us far beyond the date of Allenby's retirement from his command, up to which his chief concern had been his relations with the Turkish authorities. The territories from which they had been driven out—Mesopotamia, Syria, and Palestine—were in a chaotic state. The vast majority of the prisoners of war, though sometimes in a condition which would normally have made their movement undesirable, had to be handed over and sent home. The commander-in-chief had experts to handle problems such as the depreciated currency, but being a thorough man, he went into every detail personally. Mustapha Kemal was never easy to deal with, but his successor, Nihad Pasha, commanding the Second Army, proved even less so. He started by pretending that the terms of the armistice had not been communicated to him, then attempted to evade them by leaving behind him large numbers of troops camouflaged as gendarmerie. Allenby remained cool but firm, and before the end of 1918 Nihad had withdrawn his Second Army as ordered. Its demobilization began soon afterwards. Even these domestic measures were hindered by the French, though in this case perhaps not intentionally. Having previously landed an Armenian battalion at Alexandretta, they now put ashore two more on the opposite side of the gulf at Mersin. These troops were supposed to help in the process of pushing Nihad along; in fact, the only effect of their presence was to exacerbate the hostility between Turks and Armenians—a hostility which was due to the fact that vast numbers of the Armenians had been massacred in the course of the war and also that considerable numbers had fought, not without honor, in the Russian army under Yudenich in Caucasia. The Armenian troops had finally to be replaced by British and moved to central points, where their presence was less provocative.

Allenby's authority now extended beyond the Turkish forces with which he had been engaged and included the Sixth Army, beaten in Mesopotamia, which he had to supervise in its repatriation. Here he came up against a third Turkish general, more expert in procrastination than even the other two. Ali Ishan Pasha had won a high reputation and had probably prolonged resistance in that theater. He not only played the same game as Nihad by maintaining soldiers as gendarmerie but held up the withdrawal till the road through Diyarbekir became virtually impassable in winter, and then coolly demanded that his troops should be sent home by rail through Aleppo. He, or men on his staff, also spread anti-British and anti-Armenian propaganda whenever possible, and the British commander-in-chief had to face the probability that the atrocious massacres of Armenians which had taken place during the war would be resumed, with the Turkish soldier disclaiming all responsibility just as the Turkish statesman Talaat Pasha had done before.

Allenby therefore issued orders for the occupation of a number of towns north of the Baghdad Railway, including Urfa, and of Marash, roughly one hundred miles NNW. of Aleppo. Two towns were taken over before the year 1918 was out, but the difficulties of supply prevented the arrival of Indian troops of the 28th Brigade at Urfa till the latter half of March. Meanwhile Allenby had visited Constantinople—

where Major-General G. F. Milne, the commander of the British Salonika Army, had set up his headquarters at the military school—to submit a stern warning to the Turkish Government itself and to demand the suspension of Ali Ishan. The ministers promised to do their best and in fact did withdraw this officer who was causing so much trouble—which created a change for the better, and the regular demobilization of the Sixth Army was resumed. Yet Allenby must have sensed that these men were losing power, though he can scarcely have guessed that their end was so near, that the Turkish sultanate was so soon to disappear after having been established in Constantinople since the fifteenth century, or that the dictatorship of Mustapha Kemal was to replace the sultanate, in the new capital of Ankara.

Milne was considerably junior to Allenby, but it must not be supposed that the latter relieved him of any of his natural responsibilities. In fact, by far the heaviest task as regards the Turkish army fell to Milne, who had to disarm and reduce the great bulk of the 400,000 Turkish troops. A reasonable number had to be kept to maintain internal order as well as in the role of watching the frontiers. Turkey was allowed to keep as many as twenty divisions, but they were on a miniature scale, with a very small establishment of artillery and machine guns. Though there was the now familiar obstructionism, the work went well, even Kemal sending in large quantities of machine guns, the breechblocks of cannon, and the bolts of rifles. Disarmament was carried out in this form mainly because it was probable that a peace treaty would shortly be signed and that under its terms Turkey would be allowed to keep the greater part of her armament—though the difficulty of moving it was also a factor. How short was the vision of the political aspect! These breechblocks and cannon, the rifles and bolts, were in many cases to be brought together again by Kemal. Yet Milne could at this stage not have foreseen the future any more than Allenby.

It was Milne, too, who had to deal with General Franchet d'Espèrey to a greater extent than Allenby. The French commander-in-chief of the former Armées Alliées en Orient had been given general command of all forces in the Balkans, including European Turkey. If we read British messages, we may conclude that his postwar policy won various advantages for France, but if we turn to his biography and his letters addressed to friends at home we shall learn that he felt himself unable to maintain any such policy, that Clemenceau and Foch let him down, and that British views prevailed. He and Milne had been good friends during the war and the British general admired the great French soldier, with the result that the two men, both notoriously irascible, kept their tempers in all their difficult dealings. Finally d'Espèrey suggested to the Minister of War that the Allied command in the East in his hands should be brought to an end, and this was done late in 1920.

The most immediate benefit which Britain derived from the Mandate of Palestine was its value as a link in air travel, particularly to South Africa and India. The gentle grassy slopes southeast of the dunes about Gaza made an ideal landing place for the aircraft of those days. Throughout the period between the two World Wars passengers from the Cape to England came north to the Mediterranean in several stages, at one of which they slept the night, and then commonly transferred to a flying boat which bore them to the south of France. The Suez Canal had since its opening been regarded as vital to the United Kingdom as a short cut to India, and remained so in peace and as long as it could be kept open in the Second World War. Southern Palestine, linked with Iraq, fulfilled a similar function for air traffic. Its value was all the greater because throughout the period mentioned there was continual unrest in Egypt and always a possibility that landings in that country might be endangered. Not till after the Second World War did it become certain that the developing endurance of aircraft would render a stop in Palestine unnecessary.

It has been mentioned that when Lord Plumer was Governor of Palestine he had no troops at his disposal. The nearest land forces in his time were armored cars of the Royal Air

Force in Trans-Jordan, and they had their hands full in dealing with the Wahabis of Ibn Saud. There can be no doubt whatever that, but for the bombing by the aircraft and the ground attacks of the cars, Ibn Saub would have overrun Trans-Jordan as he had already overrun the Hejaz and was to overrun the Yemen.

Then, though Palestine had virtually nothing but citrus fruit to contribute to the British economy—which would have come, anyhow, as it had come when the Turks ruled the country—refueling and maintenance were for long invaluable on the air route to Iraq, which was a far more important contributor. The protection of the Anglo-Persian oil installations on Abadan Island in the Persian Gulf had begun the war in the Mesopotamian theater. They had been secured in 1914, and in the following year the Turks had been chased away from the wells themselves at Ahwaz, so that neither they nor the pipeline to the Shatt-al-Arab were ever again threatened throughout the war. The end of the war in Mesopotamia had witnessed an undignified rush to secure Mosul, with its oil potential, before the Turkish armistice came into force. Mosul was actually not secured until after the armistice had been signed and the legality of its occupation was more than dubious. "But the British were going to have Mosul. In the end the matter was amicably settled. The Turks marched out and the British marched in."[2]

Needless to say, having secured an oilfield which could not be protected from the sea like that of Ahwaz, the British had to protect it by aircraft, not only by means of the power to bomb an assailant but by transporting troops, the latter means of defense becoming more and more important as aircraft increased in size and carrying capacity. Into the bargain, Iraq was a protegé and, until the bloody extinction of the Hashemite kingdom after the Second World War, a very faithful friend. It is thus clear that the victory in Palestine brought very large benefits in its train from the point of view of Britain's position in the Middle East.

This writer is a warm admirer of the modern State of

Israel. At Oxford his military lectures were attended by a very young Israeli officer who had already established himself as something of a genius in warfare and was to go higher yet, who was kind enough—and one hopes he spoke the truth—to declare that he had derived benefit from them. There were many Zionists among his Jewish friends. He trusts he can say that he has never been anti-Jewish or pro-Arab in this controversy.

It is not anti-Jewish to tell the truth, which is that the conflict between the Balfour Declaration and the pledges to the Arabs brought about a most adverse and painful situation for Britain. This was not confined to Palestine by any means. It became international, particularly affecting for the worse the relations between the United Kingdom and the United States. The Jews in general bear no guilt for it, though a section of extremists exacerbated it. The blame for the impasse falls on Britain.

The Balfour Declaration—a statement by the Secretary of State for Foreign Affairs to Lord Rothschild on November 9, 1917—ran as follows: "His Majesty's Government view with favour the establishment in Palestine of a national home for the Jewish people and will use their best endeavours to facilitate the achievement of this object, it being clearly understood that nothing shall be done which may prejudice the civil and religious rights of existing non-Jewish communities in Palestine, or the rights and political status enjoyed by Jews in any other country."

The policy was to win Jewish sympathy, especially in the British Isles, Russia—still precariously a combatant—and the United States; and the money power of international Jewry was naturally not overlooked. No one was quicker to see the importance of the move than the Germans, who immediately afterwards took counsel with the Turks to see if it were possible to produce a scheme equally attractive to Zionists. A German-Jewish society, *Vereinigung Jüdischer Organisationen Deutschlands zur Wahrung Der Rechte des Osten*, was set up, and Talaat Pasha gave it some indefinite support. The scheme never took on and of course collapsed in the autumn of 1918.

The British felt that they had fortified their position. Lord Robert Cecil, Balfour's subordinate at the Foreign Office, was told by the distinguished Zionist, Chaim Weizmann, that a Jewish Palestine would be a safeguard to the Suez Canal. Churchill, speaking a couple of years before the Second World War, scoffed at the belief that the action taken sprang from quixotry or philanthrophy; on the contrary, the object was to promote victory. Few realized as yet that the change of a word in a phrase might be dynamite. When Weizmann spoke of a Jewish Palestine he made no mention of the fact that the rights of the Arabs had been guaranteed, though he personally was prepared to deal more tenderly with them than were many others. In the British Government there was no man so militantly enthusiastic as Churchill in favor of Jewish settlement; but he, when Secretary of State for the Colonies, told an Arab deputation that Britain would never tolerate the expropriation of one people by another. This was only a few years after the First World War.

The brightest moment came in 1923, when the British Mandate was confirmed and adopted by the League of Nations. The so-called "Mandatory Instrument" in no way infringed the pledges to the Arabs, and—looking back, it seems to us almost miraculous—Weizmann signed an agreement with Feisal, in virtue of which the Arabs agreed to the Balfour Declaration and to Jewish immigration, with the natural reservation that Arab independence should be retained. Prospects were never again to be so promising.

Two fresh problems now began to raise their heads. In the first place both the United Kingdom and the United States began to fear that something amounting to a dual nationality would appear on a large scale among their Jewish citizens. Thousands of Jews shared their anxiety. In all their tribulations the Jews had been good citizens in the lands of their adoption. To take their most illustrious family as an example, no one could imagine that the British and French Rothschilds would now or in the future ever be anything else. Secondly, it was dawning upon the two governments that Palestine, a country about the size of Wales and relatively thickly inhabited, was not nearly big enough for the aspirations of the Zionists or indeed for the rate of immigration and the Jewish program for the future, and that such plans as had been examined for the establishment of other settlements would fail in face of local objections, of unsuitability, or of the refusal of the Zionist leaders to consider them. The obvious deduction was that in course of time the immigrants would swamp the Arabs and that a demand for a Jewish state would gather overwhelming strength. It was, in fact, already beginning to do so.

Before the Second World War an Arab revolt of a nature never previously experienced broke out. British troops had to be rushed in on a large scale. The Arabs were now even better armed than when they had, as here recorded, collected thousands of Turkish rifles in the wake of Allenby's advance, and they were prepared to use them on a far greater scale. They were gradually worn down, but the rebellion had not been mastered when the Second World War broke out. This changed the situation completely. The Jewish settlers had, of course, every reason to support Britain, since her defeat would have led to their extermination and, even if final defeat had been staved off, the defeat of Auchinleck or Montgomery at Alamein would have sufficed to bring this about. The Arabs of Palestine were in the main also backers of the cause of the West.

Then the tension heightened once more. At the beginning of 1947 the British made what was to be virtually their last attempt at conciliation. They proposed to allow the admission to the country of four thousand Jews a month over a period of two years and after that as many as it could reasonably absorb. The Jewish Agency denounced the offer without hesitation. It was now determined to delay the foundation of a Jewish state not a day after it was strong enough to stand. The Agency was receiving financial support from various parts of the world, but more from the Jews of the United

States, perhaps those of New York alone, than from all other sources combined.

Finally the worst stage short of open war was reached. British naval patrols in the Mediterranean sought out shiploads of Jews making for Palestine without papers, took them off when the ships were caught, and held them interned in camps surrounded by barbed wire in Cyprus. Before the end of 1945 an underground Jewish rebellion against the Mandatory Government had begun. It was not a three-sided war because the Arabs did not attack the British troops, but in every other case it brought anarchy. Finally the government, carried away by the Secretary of State for Foreign Affairs, Ernest Bevin, who was disgusted with the whole business, abandoned the Mandate and the last British troops embarked at Haifa on June 30, 1948. At home the aftermath was tragic. The disgraceful anti-Jewish riots in the working-class quarters of the cities, London above all, were as often as not led by young short-time conscript soldiers who had served in Palestine and had since been demobilized. They were all the more prejudiced because they had liked and admired the highly disciplined forces of Jordan.

The United States immediately recognized the State of Israel which had been proclaimed some hours before the Mandate ended. The earliest phase of the Jewish-Arab contest had been more or less underground warfare. The next, beginning before the last detachment of British troops guarding the docks of Haifa had embarked, was very much more serious. It was the invasion of Israel by the neighboring Arab states which began in mid-May 1948. The Lebanese hardly counted, but the Syrians were very much more numerous and rather better soldiers. Egypt had a larger army still and one with equipment superior to that of the Israelis, but the officers were bad, with brilliant exceptions such as the young Nasser, and the rank and file were inclined to panic when in a tight place, beside being slow-footed when their situation was favorable. The best of the invading forces was that of Jordan. Highly trained, a proportion having served with credit in the Second

World War, they rode the storm in which their allies were wrecked with supreme confidence and ended up in possession of a large slice of the Judaean hills, which Abdullah, many thought unwisely, added to his realm. They were, however, so few in numbers that it was probably to their good fortune never to have come up against a major proportion of the Israeli army. (Its leaders said afterwards that they respected the Jordanians but would have liked to have had a full crack at them.) Their greatest feat was the capture of the Old City of Jerusalem, which remains split to this day. The Iraqi contingent, despite the warnings of British and Arab officers of the Jordanian Arab Legion, wasted its fair fighting qualities by attempting to cross the Jordan opposite Beisan at a time when it had only been able to bring its advanced guard across the desert.

It was the Egyptians who made the deepest penetration. One column moved by way of Beersheba and Hebron to Bethlehem, from which a small body pushed to a point southwest of Jerusalem; the other column made an equivalent advance along the coast road through Gaza—retained at the armistice—but the mobile columns of Israelis between the two columns acted aggressively against their inner flanks and were never eliminated. The Egyptian advance came to an end with a truce on June 11, and thenceforth the balance swung over to the outnumbered Israeli defenders.

The rest of the war requires only a few words in this context. On balance the four weeks' truce probably benefited Israel the more, but, though the Arabs asserted that this was so, they, too, were certainly glad of the breather afforded by the efforts of Count Bernadotte in his capacity as representative of the United Nations. The Arabs were, however, sufficiently confident, as on the map they had every right to be, to refuse to renew the truce.

There followed a brief but packed period of fighting on all fronts known as the "Ten Days' Offensive." In this the Israelis showed great skill in shifting forces from one front to another. On the whole they gained successes at all points except when they encountered the crack forces of Jordan. Though Britain had yielded to American and world opinion in withdrawing her officers from the actual fighting, it seemed to make little difference to the military qualities of the Arab Legion. When the second truce took place on July 18, Glubb Pasha could claim that the Legion had never lost a yard of ground which he had directed it to hold.

This second truce was actually no more than a "cease-fire," neither side expecting it to last, though it did last longer than the first. The October fighting went in favor of Israel not only on land but at sea, in which element her little navy gained a victory off Gaza and the Egyptians lost three small warships. The final offensive in Sinai was conducted by that young officer mentioned as attending the writer's Oxford lectures and would have ended in a crushing victory had Egypt not demanded an armistice in January 1949. Count Bernadotte had been murdered by the Jewish terrorist party known politely as the "Stern Group" and less politely as the "Stern Gang" and was succeeded by an American Negro, Dr. Ralph Bunche, who had been his assistant and who had been working with all his might to bring the ruinous conflict to an end. Britain was particularly glad to see it end because she had a treaty with Egypt, and the Israelis had at one stage crossed the Egyptian frontier into Sinai.

The last serious fighting—as apart from sporadic raids and counter-raids between Israelis on the one hand and Egyptians, Jordanians, and Syrians on the other—occurred in 1956. Its special interest is, first, the remarkable strides made by the Israeli army since the previous war, and secondly, the fact that it coincided with the Anglo-French attempt to secure the Suez Canal. It may be doubted whether a desert war on a considerable scale has ever been so quickly concluded. The war began with a night attack on October 29, 1956, and came to an end early on November 5 with the complete conquest of the Sinai Peninsula. It need hardly be added that Israel had to abandon her gains; nor is it necessary to point out to English and American readers that this offensive, combined with the

allied landing at Port Said, brought Anglo-American relations
to their lowest ebb in modern times.

The events briefly recorded must in greater or lesser
degree be considered as the aftermath of the campaign of
Armageddon. They far exceed in their disastrous effects any
of the benefits earlier claimed. Yet the future and even the
present are less black than they might have been. British relations with Israel are good, despite the continued Anglo-Jorda-
nian alliance, while relations with Egypt are slowly improving.
The Anglo-American wounds have been healed. It is of course
impossible to foresee how the conflict of views between
Israel and the Arab powers will develop, but even here prospects are slightly better. At our most optimistic, however, we
cannot look forward to an early, still less to a lasting, peace
between Israel and the Arab states, divided as they are by a
growing gulf of prejudice, religion, and ideology in general.
Among the worst barriers is that of the Jordanian possession
of the Old City of Jerusalem and its holding in the Jordan hills.
This not only exasperates Israel but attaches to the Kingdom of
the Jordan the section of the Arabs which is most turbulent
and unruly, as well as least well affected to Jordan rule. Their
influence is linked with that of Palestinian Arabs who have fled
to Jordan, and have already on more than one occasion put the
state in deadly peril. It is these men who are responsible for the
murder of King Abdullah and who have made several attempts
on the life of his grandson, King Hussein.

The other sore is that created by the many thousands of
Arab refugees who escaped with nothing but the clothes on
their backs. Their miseries have been alleviated to some extent
by the construction of little stone cottages to replace the
wooden shacks in which all were housed to begin with. They
are, however, fed almost entirely by UNRRA, on a marginal
diet which barely keeps them in health, though this well-man-
aged and enthusiastic agency has made creditable efforts to
provide special food for the children and to educate them in
trades and professions. It is, however, handicapped by the ill
faith of many of its subscribers, who, having raved about the

refugees' plight and urged that more must be done for them, fail to pay their dues in part, and on many occasions have paid nothing. By far the greatest part of the financial burden is borne by the United States, with Britain coming second.

Here the lack of generosity and sense of unity among the Arabs is most apparent. It has been calculated that Syria alone could absorb all the refugees in the Jordan Valley, but the Arab states together still admit only a trickle. Men trained as engineers and artisans find a fair number of jobs in the rich oil-producing lands of the Persian Gulf, but the total exodus does not keep pace with the high birthrate.

How distressing all this would have appeared to Allenby! He it was who in 1922 with the greatest difficulty wrung from Austen Chamberlain, a man in other respects tolerant and generous, the abandonment of the British protectorate and the independence of Egypt.

NOTES

NOTES

CHAPTER 1

1. Falls, *Egypt and Palestine,* vol. I, p. 9.
2. *Ibid.,* p. 26.
3. Falls, *The Great War,* p. 162.
4. *Ibid.,* p. 376.
5. Falls, *Egypt and Palestine,* vol. I, pp. 317–20.
6. Edmonds, *A Short History of World War I,* p. 234.
7. Wavell, *Allenby, Soldier and Statesman,* p. 61.
8. Kress, *Mit den Türken zum Suezkanal,* p. 265.
9. Schwarte, *Der Grosse Krieg,* p. 476.
10. Jones, *The War in the Air,* p. 209.
11. Gullett, *The Australian Imperial Force in Sinai and Palestine,* p. 678.

CHAPTER 2

1. Falls, *Macedonia,* vol. II, pp. 243–46; *The Great War,* pp. 383–85.
2. Falls, *Egypt and Palestine,* vol. II, p. 326.
3. Liman, *Fünf Jahre Türkei,* p. 309.
4. Gullett, *op. cit.,* p. 680.
5. Falls, *Egypt and Palestine,* vol. II, p. 452.
6. *Ibid.,* p. 2. The term was in origin philological and stood for the likeness of the Turkish, Magyar, and Finnish tongues. The word "Turan" is Persian and had been applied to the steppes of Central Asia.
7. *Ibid.,* p. 446.
8. Liman, *op. cit.,* p. 327.
9. Falls, *Egypt and Palestine,* vol. II, pp. 429–34.
10. Liman, *op. cit.,* p. 319.
11. *Ibid.,* p. 242.

CHAPTER 3

1. Falls, *The Great War*, p. 400.
2. Wavell, *The Palestine Campaign*, p. 205.
3. Jones, *op. cit.*, p. 209.
4. Wavell, *Allenby, Soldier and Statesman*, p. 227.
5. *Ibid.*, p. 184.
6. Falls, *Egypt and Palestine*, vol. I, p. 86.
7. Gullett, *op. cit.*, p. 256.
8. *Ibid.*, p. 354.
9. Lawrence, *Revolt in the Desert*, p. 324.
10. Larcher, *La Guerre Turque dans la Guerre Mondiale*, p. 298.

CHAPTER 4

1. Falls, *Egypt and Palestine*, vol. II, p. 484.
2. Gullett, *op. cit.*, p. 699.
3. Jones, *op. cit.*, pp. 214–21.
4. Simon-Eberhard, *Mit dem Asienkorps zur Palestina Front*, p. 107.
5. Falls, *Egypt and Palestine*, vol. II, p. 495; Liman, *op. cit.*, p. 347.
6. Liman, *op. cit.*, p. 353.
7. Jones, *op. cit.*, p. 224.
8. Gullett, *op. cit.*, p. 702.
9. Falls, *Egypt and Palestine*, vol. II, p. 508.
10. *Ibid.*, p. 503.
11. Preston, *The Desert Mounted Corps*, p. 214.
12. Falls, *Egypt and Palestine*, vol. II, p. 635.

CHAPTER 5

1. Falls, *Egypt and Palestine*, vol. II, p. 515.

2. Liman, *op. cit.*, pp. 350, 354.
3. Falls, *Egypt and Palestine*, vol. II, pp. X, 518.
4. Liman, *op. cit.*, p. 357.
5. Gullett, *op. cit.*, p. 697.
6. *Ibid.*, p. 380.
7. Falls, *Egypt and Palestine*, vol. II, p. 530.
8. Gullett, *op. cit.*, p. 707.
9. Preston, *op. cit.*, p. 231.
10. Liman, *op. cit.*, pp. 358–64.
11. Simon-Eberhard, *op. cit.*, p. 112.
12. Preston, *op. cit.*, p. 231.
13. Simon-Eberhard, *op. cit.*, p. 115.
14. Falls, *Egypt and Palestine*, vol. II, pp. 538–42.
15. Schwarte, *op. cit.*, p. 481.
16. Preston, *op. cit.*, p. 251.
17. Gullett, *op. cit.*, p. 736.

CHAPTER 6

1. Falls, *Egypt and Palestine*, vol. II, p. 554.
2. Jones, *op. cit.*, p. 231.
3. Gullett, *op. cit.*, p. 725.
4. Falls, *Egypt and Palestine*, vol. II, p. 556.
5. Gullett, *op. cit.*, p. 725.
6. *Ibid.*, p. 727.
7. Falls, *Egypt and Palestine*, vol. II, p. 558.

CHAPTER 7

1. Lawrence, *The Seven Pillars of Wisdom*, p. 475.
2. Beraud-Villars, *T. E. Lawrence*, p. 183; Nutting, *Lawrence of Arabia*, p. 112.
3. Lawrence, *Revolt in the Desert*, p. 259.
4. Hart, *T. E. Lawrence, in Arabia and After*, p. 336.
5. *Ibid.*, p. 346.
6. Liman, *op. cit.*, p. 372.

7. Falls, *Egypt and Palestine,* vol. II, p. 566.
8. Beraud-Villars, *op. cit.,* p. 289.
9. Hart, *op. cit.,* p. 351.
10. Falls, *Egypt and Palestine,* vol. II, p. 567.
11. Lawrence, *Revolt in the Desert,* p. 410.
12. Beraud-Villars, *op. cit.,* p. 240.
13. Hart, *op. cit.,* p. 357.

CHAPTER 8

1. Falls, *Egypt and Palestine,* vol. II, p. 294.
2. *Ibid.,* p. 562.
3. Schwarte, *op. cit.,* p. 481.
4. Gullett, *op. cit.,* p. 740.
5. Falls, *Egypt and Palestine,* vol. II, p. 568.
6. Liman, *op. cit.,* p. 376.
7. Falls, *Egypt and Palestine,* vol. II, p. 571.
8. *Ibid.,* pp. 577–80.
9. Hart, *op. cit.,* p. 354.
10. Gullett, *op. cit.,* p. 744.
11. Lawrence, *Revolt in the Desert,* p. 417.
12. Nutting, *Lawrence of Arabia,* p. 164.
13. Wavell, *Allenby, Soldier and Statesman,* p. 241.
14. Falls, *Egypt and Palestine,* vol. II, p. 583.
15. Lawrence, *Revolt in the Desert,* p. 422.
16. Falls, *Egypt and Palestine,* vol. II, p. 587.
17. Gullett, *op. cit.,* p. 755.
18. Hart, *op. cit.,* p. 366.
19. Falls, *Egypt and Palestine,* vol. II, p. 591.
20. Gullett, *op. cit.,* p. 762.

CHAPTER 9

1. Liman, *op. cit.,* p. 370; Hart, *op. cit.,* p. 368.
2. Beraud-Villars, *op. cit.,* p. 244.
3. Falls, *Egypt and Palestine,* vol. II, p. 598.
4. Lawrence, *Revolt in the Desert,* p. 434.
5. Falls, *Egypt and Palestine,* vol. II, p. 398.
6. *Ibid.,* p. 608.
7. Falls, *The Great War,* p. 396.
8. Gullett, *op. cit.,* pp. 729, 774.
9. Nutting, *op. cit.,* p. 174.
10. Hart, *op. cit.,* p. 385.
11. Nutting, *op. cit.,* p. 191.
12. Beraud-Villars, *op. cit.,* p. 289.

CHAPTER 10

1. Jones, *op. cit.,* p. 236.
2. Falls, *Egypt and Palestine,* vol. II, p. 605.
3. *Ibid.,* p. 606.
4. Gullett, *op. cit.,* p. 777.
5. Falls, *Egypt and Palestine,* vol. II, p. 10.
6. Gullett, *op. cit.,* p. 778.
7. Liman, *op. cit.,* p. 396.
8. Falls, *Egypt and Palestine,* vol. II, p. 614.
9. *Ibid.,* p. 616.
10. Larcher, *op. cit.,* p. 540.
11. Edmonds, *op. cit.,* p. 376.
12. Liman, *op. cit.,* pp. 399–406.
13. Gullett, *op. cit.,* pp. 787–91.

CHAPTER 11

1. Falls, *Egypt and Palestine,* vol. II, p. 296.

2. Hart, *op. cit.*, p. 283.

3. Wavell, *Allenby, Soldier and Statesman*, p. 240.

4. Gullett, *op. cit.*, p. 646.

5. Falls, *Egypt and Palestine*, vol. II, p. 636.

6. Gullett, *op. cit.*, p. 503.

7. Falls, *Egypt and Palestine*, vol. II, p. 633.

8. Falls, *The Great War*, pp. 133–36.

CHAPTER 12

1. Feiling, *A History of England*, pp. 1085, 1101.

2. Falls, *The Great War*, p. 406.

BIBLIOGRAPHY
& INDEX

BIBLIOGRAPHY

BERAUD-VILLARS, JEAN: *T. E. Lawrence*. London: Sidgwick & Jackson.

BLENKINSOP, MAJOR-GENERAL SIR L. S., and RAINEY, LIEUTENANT-COL-
ONEL J. W.: *Veterinary Services*. London: H. M. Stationery Office.

EDMONDS, BRIGADIER-GENERAL SIR JAMES E.: *A Short History of World
War I*. London: Oxford University Press.

FALLS, CAPTAIN CYRIL: *The Great War*. New York: Putnam.

—— *Military Operations: Egypt and Palestine*. London: H. M. Stationery Office.

—— *Military Operations: Macedonia*. London: H. M. Stationery Office.

FEILING, KEITH: *A History of England*. London: Macmillan.

GULLETT, H. S.: *The Australian Imperial Force in Sinai and Palestine*.
Sidney: Angus & Robertson.

HART, LIDDELL: *T. E. Lawrence, in Arabia and After*. London: Cape.

JONES, H. A.: *The War in the Air*, vol. V. Oxford: Clarendon Press.

KRESS VON KRESSENSTEIN, FRIEDRICH FREIHERR: *Mit den Türken zum Suezkanal*. Berlin: Schlegel.

KUHL, HERMANN VON: *Der Weltkrieg*, vol. II. Berlin: Kolk.

LARCHER, COMMANDANT M.: *La Guerre Turque dans la Guerre Mondiale*.
Paris: Chiron.

LAWRENCE, T. E.: *Revolt in the Desert*. London: Cape.

—— *The Seven Pillars of Wisdom*. Privately printed.

LIMAN VON SANDERS, GENERAL DER KAVALLERIE: *Fünf Jahre Türkei*. Berlin: Scherl.

NUTTING ANTHONY: *Lawrence of Arabia.* London: Hollis & Carter.

PRESTON, LIEUTENANT-COLONEL THE HON. R. M. P.: *The Desert Mounted Corps.* London: Constable.

SCHWARTE, M.: *De Grosse Krieg,* vol. IV. Leipzig: Barth.

SIMON-EBERHARD, MAX: *Mit dem Asienkorps zur Palestina Front.* Oldenburg: Stalling.

WAVELL, GENERAL SIR ARCHIBALD: *Allenby, Soldier and Statesman.* London: Harrap.

—— Colonel A. P.; *The Palestine Campaign.* London: Harrap.

INDEX